If These WALLS *Could* TALK:
KANSAS CITY ROYALS

*Stories from the
Kansas City Royals Dugout,
Locker Room, and Press Box*

Jeff Montgomery with Matt Fulks

TRIUMPH
BOOKS

Library of Congress Cataloging-in-Publication Data
Names: Montgomery, Jeff, author. | Fulks, Matt, author.
Title: If these walls could talk, Kansas City Royals : stories from the
  Kansas City Royals dugout, locker room, and press box / by Jeff Montgomery
  with Matt Fulks.
Description: Chicago, Illinois : Triumph Books, 2017.
Identifiers: LCCN 2016048514 | ISBN 9781629373843 (paperback)
Subjects: LCSH: Kansas City Royals (Baseball team)—History. | Kansas City
  Royals (Baseball team)—Anecdotes. | BISAC: SPORTS & RECREATION /
  Baseball / General. | TRAVEL / United States / Midwest / West North
  Central (IA, KS, MN, MO, ND, NE, SD).
Classification: LCC GV875.K3 M66 2017 | DDC 796.357/6409778411—dc23
LC record available at https://lccn.loc.gov/2016048514

This book is available in quantity at special discounts for your group or organization. For further information, contact:

Triumph Books LLC
814 North Franklin Street
Chicago, Illinois 60610
(312) 337–0747
www.triumphbooks.com

Printed in U.S.A.
ISBN: 978-1-62937-384-3
Design by Amy Carter

I dedicate this book to baseball fans, especially those who call themselves Royals fans. Anyone who is fortunate enough to have a career in baseball should feel indebted to its fans. I am one who certainly does. Also, to my family, who helped make my career a reality and supported me throughout. My wife, Tina, was there through the tough times in the minor leagues, and my career in the big leagues would not have been possible without her support as she had to be both Mom and Dad to our four children, Ashleigh, Connor, Spencer, and Katy. I dedicate this book also to my wonderful parents, Tom and Mary, who were both so influential in my life as a child and as an adult. And to Tina's parents, Jim and Bonnie, who helped us in so many ways during my career.

To Yordano Ventura, a great talent, who left us all too soon.

CONTENTS

FOREWORD

Three hundred is a milestone number in baseball. If a major league hitter bats .300 for his career, they say he has Hall of Fame numbers. If a pitcher gets 300 wins, he's had a Hall of Fame career. Fewer than 10 players are in the 300 home runs/300 stolen bases club. And only 27 pitchers in our game's history have saved at least 300 games. You're about to read a book from the 10th person to reach that milestone and the first one to get all 300 with the same team: our own Jeff Montgomery.

"Monty," as everyone calls him, bridges Kansas City's two World Series championship teams of 1985 and 2015. When he first came to Kansas City before the 1988 season in a trade with the Cincinnati Reds, many of the '85 Royals were Monty's teammates, including George Brett, Mark Gubicza, Bret Saberhagen, Frank White, and Willie Wilson. Then, as a broadcaster since 2010, he's been around the recent Royals, especially the 2015 team, on a daily basis.

Jeff spends a lot of time with the current Royals, and I think they respect him not only as a former player, but also because he's relatable for many of them. As a player Monty combined his God-given ability with dogged determination to record the final outs of the game. If you took the best of Greg Holland and the best of Joakim Soria, you'd have Jeff Montgomery. Like Soria, Monty had four outstanding pitches that he could—and would—use at any point to any batter. You'll read a story later in the book about when Monty threw an unexpected pitch to one of the game's most feared hitters at the time, Mo Vaughn, in a crucial situation. And like Holly, Monty was an undersized player from a smaller college who wasn't necessarily viewed as a top prospect. But through his physical preparedness and mental approach, he became one of the best closers in Royals history.

Monty and his predecessor, Dan Quisenberry, set the precedent for great closers in Kansas City. What we've seen during the past few seasons with dominating closers in Holland and Wade Davis can be traced back to Quiz and Monty.

As a longtime Royals fan, I'd admired Monty's playing career from afar. To get 304 saves, including 45 in 1993, requires incredible consistency and durability. Monty gave his managers, coaches, teammates, and Royals fans both of those things for a dozen years in Kansas City.

You'll read later in the book that Monty and I got to know each other shortly after I became the Royals general manager in June 2006. We'd see each other at Kauffman Stadium, of course, but we also lived in the same neighborhood and we'd see each other while we were out jogging. It was obvious then—as it remains now—that besides being a great player he's an even better person. Monty cares deeply about the people around him. Ask anyone who played with Monty or has worked with him as a broadcaster, and they'll tell you that he is a great teammate and leader. Those qualities won't necessarily come out on the following pages, but what you will get out of what you're about to read is a collection of fun and insightful stories from one of the best Royals of all time.

—Dayton Moore
Royals general manager

INTRODUCTION

Jeff Montgomery and I came to the Kansas City Royals in the same year—1988—Monty as a new member of the pitching staff, me as a new member of the media contingent.

Just before spring training began, Kansas City obtained him from the Cincinnati Reds for outfielder Van Snider. It turned out to be a great deal for the Royals. Snider would play just 19 games in two seasons for the Reds, his only major league experience. Monty would spend 12 years in the Royals bullpen, pitching in 686 games and recording a team-record 304 saves.

I arrived as a Royals beat writer for *The Kansas City Star* after many years in St. Louis with the *St. Louis Post-Dispatch*, *The Sporting News*, and the *St. Louis Globe-Democrat*. I'd spend the next 27 years covering the Royals for *The Star* and later MLB.com. One of the most rewarding experiences of all those years was dealing with a consummate professional athlete, an intelligent college graduate, and an all-round good guy like Jeff Montgomery. I was there when he recorded his first save in 1988 and his last in 1999.

No. 1 was the only save that Monty got in 1988, coming shortly after he was called up from Omaha. That year he was destined to work as a set-up man for closer Steve Farr. But during a home series against the Oakland A's, Farr was pressed into service as a starter for ailing Floyd Bannister, and two days later, Monty relieved Bret Saberhagen. He induced Rickey Henderson to hit into a double play in the eighth inning and then got three straight ground-outs in the ninth. It was a perfect outing on June 8, 1988, to preserve a 5–4 victory.

No. 304 came at Seattle during the same series that Monty very kindly gave me the exclusive story on news that he'd decided to retire after the season. This time Monty was the fifth pitcher of the night and he retired all four batters he faced, starting with a strikeout of Mariners outfielder Jay Buhner. It was a perfect outing on September 20, 1999, to preserve a 10–9 victory.

This is Monty's book of baseball stories, and let me offer one or two about him. Some of his other saves were not so easy. Reaching his milestone 300th save was a battle. After having as many blown saves (five) as saves, he went to Omaha for a month to rehab a sore hip before snagging the big one against the Baltimore Orioles. For all his success in the role of closer, Monty often had the knack of making his manager and Royals fans sweat and he called save No. 300 "typical."

There were two out and nobody on in the ninth inning with the Royals ahead of the Orioles 8–6 when he arrived from the bullpen. All he needed was one out. However, both Mike Bordick and B.J. Surhoff singled. Now we're talking a real save, not a gimme. Monty put himself in a jam and was pitching in peril. Then, whew, he got Albert Belle to ground out, and 300 was in the books. Interesting sidenote: Royals manager Tony Muser had been ejected from the game, and so coach Jamie Quirk, as acting manager, was the one who summoned Montgomery into the game. It's fitting because Quirk had been the catcher for Monty's first career save.

Monty wasn't how you pictured a closer in those days. He didn't wear a hard-case face like Goose Gossage or carry a Mississippi gambler aura like Rollie Fingers. He had that choirboy look, a picture of innocence. Nor did he have a fanciful nickname like Al Hrabosky's "Mad Hungarian." He was just Monty. "People have always said I don't look the part," he said.

Frank Funk, Monty's first pitching coach in Kansas City, put it this way: "When he comes into the game, they say, 'Here comes the leprechaun.'"

Instead of a blazing fastball with maybe one secondary pitch, Montgomery featured a moderate but lively fastball, a curve, a slider, and a change-up. It was a full assortment of pitches, usually kept low and on the corners. It kept hitters guessing and certainly got the job done.

And, on those infrequent occasions when things went wrong, Monty was always at his locker to face reporters. He was a stand-up guy. Although he certainly gained fame, he liked it best when he was ignored. In his words: "I've tried to be very quiet. It's a position where when the people focus their attention on me, it's normally negative. When you do your job, everybody's shaking hands, taking a shower, and going home. But when you don't do the job, there's a lot of attention because you stunk up the place."

Monty had a knack for putting things in perspective. Analyzing the job of closing in 1998, he said: "The line between being real good and real bad at this level is nearly invisible. It's so miniscule that it's very difficult to recognize it sometimes."

He also had a penchant for perseverance. He almost quit the game a couple times—once when he was stuck in the Cincinnati farm system in 1987, another time when he struggled after shoulder surgery in 1996. But he kept grinding right into the Royals Hall of Fame. Monty was humble. When he surpassed Dan Quisenberry's club record for saves at 239, he bowed to Quiz: "He will always be the premier closer."

Now Monty has some stories to throw your way. Knowing him, he'll keep you intrigued and entertained right to the very end. He's a closer, after all.

—Dick Kaegel
Former Royals beat writer
for *The Kansas City Star*

(Jeff Montgomery)

CHAPTER 1
ROYALTY

Mr. and Mrs. K

It should be a prerequisite that the first chapter of any book discussing the Royals should include Ewing and Muriel Kauffman, George Brett, and Denny Matthews. Topping that list are Mr. and Mrs. K because if not for each of them the Royals wouldn't have started in Kansas City in the first place.

The reason I say that is pretty simple because once the A's moved to Oakland after the 1967 season, Kansas City didn't have baseball. As Major League Baseball expanded for the 1969 season and granted Kansas City a team, several civic and business leaders encouraged Mr. Kauffman to buy the franchise. Mr. K wasn't a baseball fan—or a sports fan at all, really—but he loved Kansas City. As he weighed what to do, Muriel was the one to convince him to do it. Muriel had a fun personality, so I'm sure that was a lively conversation.

Throughout his time owning the Royals, Mr. Kauffman was not a real visible owner. He was at the games every night and he could be seen in his suite, but it was rare for him to be in the clubhouse or down on the field. Players from the early years say the same thing. In fact, Royals Hall of Fame pitcher Dennis Leonard told me about how the 1977 club, which won more games than any other Royals team, was mired in a losing streak. "After a doubleheader against Chicago," Leo said, "Mr. Kauffman came into the clubhouse, which he didn't do very often. I thought he was going to be chewing us out. Instead Mr. Kauffman gave us all about $250 and said, 'Take your wife out, relax, and have a good time.' We started to go on a streak during August and September where we won 10 in a row in mid-August, swapped a couple, and then won 16 in a row, lost one, and then won eight in a row. So we won 24 out of 25 games. It was phenomenal."

We didn't experience anything like that after I joined the Royals, but Mr. Kauffman would come through the clubhouse and shake everyone's hand and talk to us by name (even though I'm guessing it was

The Royals exist because of the generous Ewing Kauffman and his wife, Muriel, who convinced him to buy the Royals. *(Kansas City Royals)*

media relations director Dean Vogelaar whispering the names of the Jeff Montgomerys of the world in his ear).

Mr. Kauffman didn't have many reasons to be around the players often because his philosophy with the Royals, as with his business, was to surround himself with the best people for each area and then let them make those decisions. He did that with the Royals from the beginning, when he hired Cedric Tallis in January 1968 from the California Angels to be the Royals' first general manager. Tallis then hired baseball men, including Lou Gorman, Joe Burke, Herk Robinson, and John Schuerholz. When I arrived in 1988, Burke was the team president and Schuerholz was the general manager. (A few years later, Robinson became the GM.) It was obvious to me that Mr. Kauffman trusted those men and gave them the reins. He let them run the baseball team. Mr. K was there to take care of big picture things, write the checks, and cover what the team needed in order to be successful.

All of that's not to say that Mr. K didn't care about the club. He wanted to protect his investment, but he also wanted to win. One idea that he felt would help both areas was the formation of the Royals Baseball Academy in the early 1970s. His belief was that great athletes could learn the fundamentals in a school-like environment and develop into major league players. Overall, it's not a bad idea. In fact, many major league franchises have similar academies in various parts of the world. The Royals have a Dominican Academy, for instance, where players live and play baseball. Mr. Kauffman was a little ahead of his time, especially with the old-school baseball minds who felt the Royals Baseball Academy was a waste of time, effort, and money. Ironically, one of the biggest opponents was Cedric Tallis. If it'd been given a chance and lasted more than four years, the academy might've thrived and become another way for major league teams to find and develop players. However, the Royals Baseball Academy turned out 14 major league players, including Ron Washington, U.L. Washington, and one of the Royals greatest players, Frank White.

In the early 1990s, I got to know Mrs. K better than I knew Mr. K. I was our team's player rep from 1991 to 1999. Although one might think that would put me in front of Mr. K and our general manager more, that's not the case. Essentially, I was a mouthpiece from our New York office to our players. (Remember, it was at a different time, technologically speaking.) But as the players' rep, I presented flowers to Mrs. K on the field on Opening Day each season, so we had a little interaction that way. I got to know her really well, though, in 1992. I was at home in Cincinnati after the season, and Herk called me to let me know that Mrs. K wanted to invite Tina and me on the Lancers trip to Puerto Vallarta, Mexico. The timing couldn't have been worse. We had decided we were going to move to Kansas City full time around Thanksgiving. In addition to all that goes with a move—packing, selling a house, buying a new house, changing schools, etc.—this was especially emotional because we were leaving our home area of Cincinnati. Of course, our move was around the time of the Lancers trip. So I told Herk, "I appreciate you asking us, but we're trying to get everything ready to move. I just don't think we can make it work."

He paused for a moment and said, "Look, if Mrs. K wants you to go on the Lancers trip, you need to go on the Lancers trip." Needless to say, we made it work, thanks largely to my mom and dad, who went on the trip so they could take care of our children when Tina and I had Lancers activities. We got to know Mrs. K very well that week. I became long-time friends with a lot of the Lancers as a result of that trip.

Mrs. K was a very blunt and to-the-point lady who had a lot of fun. She wasn't mean-spirited when she spoke what was on her mind; it was just her personality. I remember only one time when directness got her in a little hot water. We were coming through customs after a series in Toronto. Mrs. K, who was from Canada, had purchased some items (furs come to mind). The customs agent made her open her luggage to show him the items. I don't remember exactly what her comment was that was frowned upon, but she wasn't exactly happy to have to open her luggage there. Let's just say that sometimes in customs: less is best.

Less than a year after that trip, on August 1, 1993, Mr. K passed away. About 18 months later, on March 17, 1995, Mrs. K passed away. They were a terrific couple who loved Kansas City and left a lasting legacy on our community. Incidentally, as we approached deadline for this book—and were working on this section—Kansas City celebrated the 100th anniversary of Mr. K's birth.

George Brett

When I first joined the Royals shortly before spring training in 1988, I didn't really know much about the organization and I definitely hadn't heard of many players. One exception to that is George Brett. One of the game's greats, he was the most visible Royals player on a national level, and I was looking forward to having him as a teammate. By that time in his career, George had made the transition to first base. In 1987 Kevin Seitzer burst onto the scene for the Royals and started playing third base, which allowed George to move to first. It was good for him health-wise because—even as hard as he played first—it took some stress off his body, especially on the artificial turf. In May 1988 the

The best Royals player ever, George Brett, kisses home plate after his last game at Royals Stadium. *(Kansas City Royals)*

Royals released Steve Balboni, which signified George was going to be playing first on a regular basis.

As I got to know George in the spring of 1988, the most pleasant surprise to me was the way he welcomed new or younger players to the Royals. A great example was when we were in Boston for a weekend series about five weeks after I'd been called up. I was being a typical rookie—the old idea of just be quiet and speak when spoken to. We had a doubleheader Friday night with a day game on Saturday. I was about to catch the team bus and head back to the hotel when George asked, "What are you doing tonight, rook?"

"I'm just going back to the hotel."

"No, you're not. You're coming with us." As a rookie if George Brett suggests you go with his group, you go with his group.

We started at the Cask 'n Flagon, a bar across from Fenway Park. I don't know how many places we went that night, but I think we beat the sunrise back to the hotel…barely. George was supposed to have Saturday's game off. We got to the ballpark, though, and whoever was going to play in George's place couldn't, so George was in the lineup. With fairly bloodshot eyes, he went out and got two hits that game, including one off the Green Monster, and two RBIs.

In many ways George's taking care of young players and making them feel as if they belonged was a small example of him being a good teammate and leader. George was single then and had a lot of friends, so he didn't need to hang out with the younger players, but I think it was good for both George and the young players. Besides, rookies made good running buddies. It wasn't restricted to going out after a game either.

When Mark Gubicza and Bret Saberhagen made the club out of spring training in 1984, they'd never been to Kansas City so they didn't know much about the area. George invited them to stay with him at his home. So the three of them became roommates for the first month or so of the season. As George told my co-author Matt Fulks for the book

100 Things Royals Fans Should Know & Do Before They Die: "Instead of putting them in a hotel near the ballpark, I had two extra bedrooms in my house, so I told them that they could stay with me until they found a place. After about three weeks, Gubie asked me if he could use the phone and get something to eat from the refrigerator. I said, 'Mark, you can use the phone anytime you want to and you can eat anything out of the refrigerator that you want.' Meanwhile, Saberhagen would come down first thing in the morning, go raid my closet, put on my clothes, and take off for the day."

George was fun to be around away from the field, but on the field, he was an intense, great leader for the Royals. He wasn't often a boisterous or rah-rah kind of guy, but young players could learn from the way he worked and prepared. George has an inner drive to get better, but his work mentality kicked in shortly before the All-Star Break in 1974. He was hitting a little better than .200 when hitting coach Charley Lau asked George if he was ready to get to work on his swing. George showed up at the stadium early afternoon the next day to start working with Charley and he continued to get there early for the better part of his career. George's batting average was .205 on June 2 and .242 at the All-Star break. He finished the 1974 season hitting .282 and was third in Rookie of the Year voting behind Mike Hargrove and Bucky Dent.

As great as he was as a teammate, George could be ornery at times. During my first spring training in 1988, the corner of our clubhouse in Florida had George, Saberhagen, Gubicza, and Steve Farr. For the most part, it was a quiet area except this one day when Tom Leathers dropped by for an interview with George. Tom Leathers was a longtime writer and publisher in Kansas City. At the time he was the publisher (and writer) of *The Squire*, which was a weekly newspaper. A year or so earlier, Leathers had written something negative about George. The day Tom walked into our clubhouse, he had a new and expensive Minolta camera hanging from his neck and a notepad in his hand. He asked George if he had a few minutes to talk for an interview. George obliged. I don't remember how long the interview went, but George was incredibly cordial and gave Tom whatever time was needed.

When they finished the interview, George starting showing a lot of interest in Tom's expensive Minolta, asking where he got it and how much it cost. George finally asked if he could look at it. Tom handed over the camera. The pleasantries were finished. George took the camera and threw it as hard as he could against a cinder block wall. That poor camera was in hundreds of pieces. Then he took Tom's notepad and started ripping up all the notes of the interview they'd just finished and threw them in the trash can. George then sat down and said, "Just send me a bill." The incident didn't go over very well in the Royals front office. In April someone paid the bill for the camera—I'm assuming George did—and the Royals issued a public apology to Tom Leathers.

George could be called "Mr. Clutch." There were so many games, especially when we were behind, that we felt all we needed to do was to get him in a situation to drive in runs and there was a good chance he'd get it done. He'd never walk through the dugout and tell guys to jump on his back, but you knew that you wanted to be in a position to jump on his back. He did that countless times in the more than 2,700 games he played in a Royals uniform during his 21-year career.

Many players get butterflies in their stomachs, especially in pressure situations, but as George has said: "I was able to get all my butterflies to fly in the right formation…I used to tell myself in pressure situations: don't try harder, try easier. I was able to alleviate a lot of tension and try easier. So it slowed everything down instead of speeding everything up."

Unfortunately, I missed the majority of George's career and most of his iconic moments when he came through in the clutch, such as his home run off New York Yankees pitcher Goose Gossage in the 1980 playoffs, the pine tar home run against Gossage in 1983, and his Game 3 performance against the Toronto Blue Jays in the 1985 playoffs. However, one moment that I saw in person during George's career that I'll never forget was the night he got his 3,000th hit against the Angels.

Anaheim was our final road stop for 1992 before we finished the season with three home games against the Minnesota Twins. That season had been a struggle for our team, so there was no hope for the postseason. Going into the series against the Angels, we were about 24 games out of first place. Things hadn't been faring much better for George, who was 39 years old. Going into that four-game series, he sat at 2,996 hits. The best place for George to get his 3,000th hit would be in Kansas City, but the second-best place would be Anaheim, which is about 30 miles east of where he grew up in El Segundo. George had a lot of friends from California and from Kansas City in Anaheim for the potential milestone, but he'd missed the first two games because of an injured right shoulder. It's easy to assume, knowing George and his career, that he'd get at least four hits in the final six games of the season, but it definitely wasn't guaranteed. On top of that, being 39 with an injured shoulder, there was no guarantee that he'd be back in 1993. Anything could happen during the offseason.

Manager Hal McRae made two lineups for the game on September 30. One without George and one with George as the designated hitter. After batting practice George told Mac that he could play. In the top of the first inning, George doubled off Angels starter Julio Valera. In the third he singled off Valera. Likewise in the fifth, he hit a line drive to center. So there he was, in typical George Brett fashion, having a 3-for-3 night midway through the game and sitting at 2,999 hits. In the seventh inning against Tim Fortugno, George hit a rocket past Ken Oberkfell at second base. The ball took a scorching hop, and there was no chance Oberkfell could get it. We were in the bullpen, and everyone ran onto the field to congratulate George. A couple minutes later, while talking with first baseman Gary Gaetti, George got picked off first.

Besides George getting four hits that night to reach 3,000, he came up again in the ninth and reached on an error, so in five plate appearances that night, he reached base five times. Rick Reed threw a complete-game shutout for us, and we beat the Angels 4–0.

After the game we went back to the Doubletree Hotel and had a big party with the team and George's friends and family. The next day I gave George a gift I'd bought him at a specialty shop. I bought George a desk clock with the inscription: "To Lou, the ultimate professional. Congratulations on number 3,000." (Lou was George's nickname, and it's the one he preferred. I believe he was called that because he loved Looney Tunes cartoons growing up.)

As it turned out, George did have one more season to get his 3,000th hit, as he played the 1993 season exclusively as our designated hitter. In 145 games George finished with 149 hits and a .266 batting average. Excluding 1973, when George came to the major leagues and played in 13 games, that .266 average was the second lowest of George's career. (His lowest was .255 two seasons earlier.) It wasn't a George Brett-level of performance, but he was still playing at a very high level. Even hitting .266 he was our best player. Frankly, nearly every Royals player from 1974 to 1993 could say that George was the best all-around, most consistent player on each of those teams. At the age of 40 in 1993, he led our team in RBIs and was second in home runs, third in runs scored, and third in hits.

So it didn't come as a surprise to anyone when, on Tuesday, January 5, 1999, it was announced that George was going to be inducted into the Baseball Hall of Fame in his first year of eligibility. That class included his good friend Robin Yount and pitcher Nolan Ryan. Coincidentally, our last series in 1993—so the last of George's career—was at Texas, where Ryan was, though he was not on the actice staff of the Rangers.

George Brett's 21-year, Hall of Fame career included 3,154 hits. *(Kansas City Royals)*

**George Brett Hall of Fame Induction
Acceptance Speech
Cooperstown, New York
July 26, 1999**

Thank you. God, Robin, you don't know how lucky you were to go first.

Thank you, Kansas City. I have been sitting in the hot seat over here for about two hours wondering if I was gonna be able to get through this thing. I saw Robin get through brilliantly and the other inductees and hopefully I'll be able to do a job as well as they have. Obviously, it's a big thrill for me to be here today. First of all, I would like to thank the Baseball Writers of America for their overwhelming support in naming me into the Hall of Fame this year. I dreamt the same way Ryan did, or Nolan did, and I dreamt the same way Robin did. And this is a dream come true.

I would also like to thank the staff of the Hall of Fame for making me and my family feel so welcome, all the kindness that you've given us. You are truly, and I mean this, you are truly the game's caretakers and you're doing a wonderful job.

It is such an honor to stand here and to be inducted with such good friends. Robin Yount, whom I played against for all those years. And I do mean that sincerely, of all the guys that I did play against for all that length of time, Robin, you are the one I enjoyed playing against the most. So congratulations to all you people in Milwaukee; you saw one of the best ballplayers I ever saw.

To Orlando Cepeda, who came over in 1974 and thought I wasn't going to make it. I'm glad you don't scout for the Royals, Orlando. And to Nolan Ryan, a guy I played against 13 years and never said boo to, and he never said boo to me either until January 6, when I met him in New York after we were announced that we were going to the Hall of Fame. And since then, Nolan, I think we've developed a little friendship, and hopefully it will grow within years.

Today concludes a long journey that has taken me from

Southern California throughout America. And I very honestly stand humbly before you today in Cooperstown. As with any journey, I have been helped by so many people. That is why this induction is so special to me. I get to stand here and thank the many, many people who have helped me over my career in many different ways, besides just playing baseball. I have always believed we live with our friends, not our accomplishments. I haven't accomplished one thing in baseball since I retired, but I still have a lot of friends. I think it all started in 1971. My high school coach, John Stevenson, I think, taught me how to be a winning ballplayer. He taught me what it's like to be on a winning team, day after day. And John, I really think that helped me through my career.

Rosie Gilhausen, the scout that signed me, who called the Kansas City Royals and said, "You know I had this little skinny shortstop, 5'10", 165 pounds, and his brother Ken's a pretty good player in the big leagues. You know, I think this guy's got a pretty good chance to be a pretty good player." And Rosie Gilhausen convinced the Royals to draft me. It wasn't an easy negotiation. I don't think when you did anything with my father, it was easy. My father, the first day he came over to the house, threw him out. And he came back a few days later and gave me a little bit more money but not much. But my brother, Bobby, gave me the best advice I had gotten that day: "If you think you're that good, what are you worrying about the money now. There's a lot more money to be made in baseball." He was right.

The managers that I played for in the major leagues were very instrumental. From Jack McKeon, I remember my rookie year, always had a smile on his face. The game wasn't life—or life or death. Dick Howser, who managed us, managed the Kansas City Royals to our first world championship in 1985 and then left us all too soon. To two old teammates I had, Duke Wathan...I played against him, I played with him in the minor leagues, I played with him in the major leagues for so long and then got a chance to play for him. Duke, I appreciate all the friendship we've had over the years. Hal McRae, whom I consider the best hitting coach in baseball right now. He's the one that taught me how to play the game of baseball. He led by example. He ran balls out, he slid into second, tried to break up double plays. He stretched singles to doubles, doubles to triples. He would do whatever it took to win a ballgame. And you know what, he wasn't in a hurry to go home when it was over. He was willing to sit in his locker, have a few cold ones, and discuss the game for as long as it took to learn something from other players or to help them learn. He was a great teammate and great man to play for.

Everybody thinks I forgot Whitey Herzog. Well, I didn't. Whitey Herzog, to this day, is a very, very special friend to me. I remember his first day, when he came over to manage the Kansas City Royals. He said, "George, you're playing third and you're hitting third every day as long as I'm managing." Prior to that I was hitting sixth or seventh or first or third; it didn't matter. But he showed some confidence in me, and that gave me stability as a major leaguer. And not only that, Whitey, all those home-cooked meals you gave me when I was single and needed a home-cooked meal once a summer. Um, the hunting trips, the fishing trips, the golf games that we had. You're a very special man.

I'd like to thank the Kansas City Royal organization for their support over so many years. I signed with them in 1971 and I'm still with 'em. Hopefully I'll be with them for a long time. To this day, I firmly believe that I am still the biggest Royal fan in the country. My owners that I've had, we had some great owners in Kansas City. Ewing and Muriel Kauffman did a tremendous job. They showed a lot of confidence in me as a youngster by giving me a five-year contract early in my career and then renegotiating that or extending that. And then we had another owner come in 1984, Avron Fogelman. Avron Fogelman and his wife, Wendy. Avron gave me the best advice I've ever been given. In 1984 he pulled me in one day and he says, "You know, you've spent 43 days on the disabled list, and I'm paying you more money than anybody else on this team." He said, "What I want you to do next year is go get yourself in the best shape you possibly can, and you come to spring training and you go out and help us win a World Series. We were capable of doing that. Sure enough, in 1984, the winter, a friend of mine from high school took off work; we worked out. I came to spring training in the best shape in my life. I got there, and everybody thought I was sick. They said, "George, you're too skinny, gain 10 pounds." Well, you know what, I gained about five back all summer, and had the best year I had, and we won the World Series.

My equipment manager, to this day, is one of my best friends, Alex Zych. I would like to thank him for treating me with such respect as an 18-year-old kid in his first big league camp. Your friendship means the world to me today, Alex.

And there's been a guy that's been family to not only myself, but to all my brothers, my mother. He's the godfather of one of our children—Arthur Richman. Thank you Arthur, who's now an executive with the New York (Yankees).

My teammates over the last 20 years that I've had, thank you for all your friendship; that's been so important to me. You all have made such an impact on my life. But not only as a player, but as a man. There is one that stands out—Jamie Quirk. Thanks.

Charley Lau was my hitting coach in 1974. At that time I was hitting .200 with 200 at-bats at the All-Star break. He put his arm around me and he said, "George, I think you got a chance to hit, but you're gonna have to change a few things." I said, "Well, what do you have in mind?" And he said, "Well, I'll tell you what, we have two days off for the All-Star break, we have practice at 5:00 on Wednesday, and then we're gonna jump on a plane and fly to Baltimore. Why don't you meet me at the stadium at 2:00 and we'll sit down and we'll discuss it and we'll try to figure out a philosophy and a theory that will work for you?" Well, we got out there and we looked at video of players that he's helped before and other players that he wanted to, maybe, model myself after. And we started to take batting practice every day. I think for as long as Charley Lau was our hitting coach, he and I had extra batting practice, 3:00 on the road, 4:00 at home. Some days it was for five swings, 10 swings, just to make sure you didn't lose anything from the day before. And some days might have been for 15, 20 minutes, trying to figure out what's happened from the night before. But Charley, thank you so much for molding me as a ballplayer and making today possible.

I ran into little Charley yesterday, and he gave me this New York Yankee ring to wear. Charley, I can't do it! (He said while laughing.) I don't like those Yankees still.

To my brothers. You know, sometimes I wonder why all this has happened to me and not you. All I ever wanted to do was be as good as you. (He said while crying.) Right now, I wish it was one of you, believe me. But I know the respect you all have for the game. And I know how hard, I know you know how hard, it really is to play. So thank you for all your support.

To my mother, Ethel. You were the heart and soul of our family growing up. Hopefully, your loving and understanding ways have rubbed off on me as Leslie and I try to raise our three boys. Thanks for being here today and in the past, Mom. I love you.

And to my father who passed away in 1992 prior to me getting 3,000 hits and right after I had gotten married. He's never seen his grandchildren—at least my three boys. But growing up, sometimes I misunderstood your tough and dominant ways, Dad. But as I've grown up, I have realized what your goals were: for me and my brothers never to be content and to be tough competitors. I think we all learned well from you. Thank you.

To my wife, Leslie, of seven years. I didn't get married, I was a bachelor playing in the major leagues 'til I was 38 years old. And I met this woman in 1990, and we ended up getting married in 1992. You are everything a wife and mother could be. You remind me so much of my mother. You made my life so much more enjoyable. And you had me from hello.

To my three boys, Jackson, Dylan, and Robin, you've given me such great joy. Whatever you choose to do in life, sons, I only hope you have the Brett work ethic. Strive to be your best, and I will always try to be there for you.

And the fans of Kansas City. When I first arrived in Kansas City in 1973, you welcomed me into your beautiful city and into your homes. It's a place where I met my wife, and my three children were born. And to this day, I'm so proud to call K.C. home. Many of you have made this trip, and I really appreciate that. I know Cooperstown is a long way from Kansas City.

Also it is my understanding right now in Kansas City, they are showing this on the Jumbotron live. And I cannot thank you people enough for going out there and supporting the Royals today and for your support over so many years.

I have so much to be thankful for, and the people of Kansas City have made it possible for me. My brother Ken played on...what, 11 or 12, 10 or 11 teams in a 12-year career? And he said he wouldn't change places with anybody because he's met so many wonderful people. Well, I've met that many wonderful people in Kansas City. So thank you.

To all my friends, who've made this trip from all over the country—from San Diego to Memphis, St. Louis, Florida, Southern California, Spokane. I even had a friend of mine fly in with his wife and two daughters from Honolulu. That's a long flight. I can't thank you enough for coming out here and, and sharing this moment with myself and my family.

And to everybody here, thank you for making this weekend such a wonderful and unforgettable night. I will never, ever forget the last three days. Thank you.

The incomparable Denny Matthews has broadcast Royals games since 1969.
(Kansas City Royals)

Denny Matthews

I was not aware of how iconic radio broadcaster Denny Matthews was when I joined the Royals in 1988, but it didn't take long to realize how great he and Fred White were together. I got to know both extremely well over the years and I can say without hesitation that—in addition to how good of broadcasters they are—they're even better people.

Not all players can say this, but as a reliever, I had a chance to listen to Denny a lot during my career. Our bullpen was near the ground crew's area, so head groundskeeper George Toma would come out of his office in the first inning and tell me, "Son, it's all yours." (George called everyone "son.") I would then go inside his office and relax while watching and listening to the game. So I got to hear a lot of Denny and Fred. At the time not many of our home games were televised, so we'd get the out-of-town TV feed and listen to our radio guys. I've probably heard Denny call more than a thousand games.

Denny is probably the most routine-oriented person in baseball, especially in the way he prepares for a broadcast. While most broadcasters have their laptops and iPads and they're pulling information instantaneously, Denny gets much of his information the old-fashioned way either through the teams' notes or newspaper articles. It's impressive. Besides that, his insight is spectacular. He played the game through college, and his knowledge helped him get the Royals job in 1969. His original partner, Buddy Blattner, hired Denny, who had no real experience in broadcasting before getting the Royals job. "That's one of the reasons I chose Denny Matthews to be my partner: he had no experience whatsoever," Blattner said. "He very much liked baseball, he was a reasonably good athlete, and he had an utterly fantastic memory." Indeed, Denny has a very keen memory, especially with meaningful moments in Royals history. To hear him tell those stories is pretty cool.

There are baseball fans out of our market who don't appreciate his style, which is understandable, because he's not a yeller and screamer like so many broadcasters today. He's old school. I'd like to think my style is more like Denny's—calm and not as excitable. My objective as a broadcaster is for the listener or viewer to learn something. The broadcaster shouldn't have to tell the listener how to feel. Denny's not there to entertain. He's there as a voice and he does a remarkable job of that. For the millions of Royals fans out there, he's much appreciated.

One thing I like about Denny is that he's to the point. As a player turned broadcaster, there's a line that broadcasters have to cross and be truthful. Sometimes that hurts. So when it came to the way I was performing—or not performing—during my last season, Denny's job was to tell it like it was. It was my job as a player to eliminate outside influences that I couldn't control, particularly the media, whether that's what the team's broadcaster might be saying, what a radio sports-talk show host is saying, or what a columnist is writing. I couldn't let any of that interfere with my job. I learned that during the minor leagues when I was in Vermont with the Cincinnati Reds' Double A affiliate. I was struggling and reading these articles about my struggles. One of the veteran players told me I'd be better off eliminating all of that. I did my best to practice that throughout the rest of my career.

Joe Posnanski, who's a national columnist now and one of the best in the business, was with *The Kansas City Star*. He wrote a column that infuriated me. I had a one-on-one with him and Steve Fink, our media relations guy. We were in the stairwell at Kauffman Stadium, and I let Joe have it. That's never been the case with Denny. Because of the respect he has for the players and the respect they have for him, a player would never want to get on the bus after a game and strangle Denny.

When I listen to other broadcasters now, I'm more analytical about what they're saying. They have an opinion for a reason, and I may learn something from them. Since I've listened to Denny more than any other broadcaster, he's influenced my thinking and my career. There have been numerous times I've heard Denny talking about something that I just witnessed, but he says something about a play or a situation that hadn't crossed my mind. Denny has an uncanny ability to extract some of those important moments. Doing TV now, I look forward to our Sundays with Denny in the booth. He's very good on TV. I'm not sure he realizes just how good he is.

I went into Royals Hall of Fame in 2003, a year before Denny was inducted. After he went in during the 2004 season, he was on the radio and made the comment about how, even though he'd introduced so many Royals into the Royals Hall of Fame, he didn't know what to expect. He said, "I talked to Monty about his, and he told me it would be very overwhelming and he was right." That comment, as small as it may seem, was huge to me.

Three years later, though, Denny deservedly received the highest honor for any baseball broadcaster when he was selected as the 2007 Ford

C. Frick Award recipient. He received his award during the Hall of Fame ceremonies when Cal Ripken Jr. and Tony Gwynn were inducted. There were an estimated 75,000 people in the small hamlet of Cooperstown on that hot Sunday afternoon.

As he's told on the air, Denny came away with some incredible stories from the weekend's festivities. He was able to meet his dad's childhood hero, Stan Musial, as well as other legends such as Sandy Koufax and Willie Mays. One of my favorite Denny stories from that weekend actually revolves around Koufax and Mays, who faced each other plenty of times during the heated Dodgers-Giants rivalry, and something Mays told Denny on the bus ride to the Clark Sports Complex for the ceremony. "I had heard that Willie was kind of sullen at times, but he turned out to be great and gave me a fascinating conversation during the 20-minute ride," Matthews said. "Among other topics I asked him how he did as a player against Koufax. He said, 'Well, I hit four home runs against him, and he never threw breaking balls against me. Then one night in San Francisco, he threw me a slider, and I hit a home run. The next day I went over and asked Sandy why he threw me a slider. He said he wanted to see if I could hit one.'"

**Denny Matthews' Ford C. Frick Award
Acceptance Speech
Cooperstown, New York
July 29, 2007**

Thank you, Tom (Seaver). Tom Terrific, what a perfect nickname because it fits the person as well as describing the pitcher. Congratulations, Cal, Tony, and Rick (Hummel). And I'm so proud of the fact that all four of us have spent our entire careers with one organization.

Ladies and gentlemen, members of the Hall of Fame, today as you bestow upon me the greatest honor a baseball broadcaster can receive, I think back to the 1983 Frick Award winner, a childhood hero of mine, Jack Brickhouse. Upon receiving the Frick Award, Jack said, "Today, I feel like a man, 60 feet, six inches tall." Half a century, a million memories since I grew up listening to Jack, I tell you what, today I know exactly how he felt.

The summer nights in Bloomington were hot and humid. I'm 10 years old, lying on the living room floor with a big pillow propped up against the big console radio, my baseball cards beside me. I'm listening to the local radio station, WJBC, one of the many stations on the Cardinals radio network, and the voices coming out of that speaker—Joe Garagiola, Jack Buck, Harry Caray, three of the best ever, together talking to me every night. Little did I know, little did they know, but they were preparing and teaching a 10-year-old boy in central Illinois how to broadcast Major League Baseball. And what marvelous teachers they were. And to think I didn't have to turn in any homework, write any term papers, pay any tuition, just lie in front of the radio each summer night and learn.

At age 10, you don't think about broadcasting. You want to play. And play we did. What beautiful summers they were, pickup games at Fell Avenue Park, Wiffle ball games in the backyard, trading baseball games with your buddies, then when it grew too dark to play, head to the radio to see how the Cardinals were doing, and when that game was over, spin the radio dial. What other games could I get from faraway cities? The quality of the radio signal was immaterial, the opportunity for education irreplaceable, so twist the dial, who do you get? Who's this Ernie Harwell? Boy, he's pretty good. Bob Prince, who does he announce for? I like him. He's funny. Chuck Thompson. Yeah, I didn't know. What game is this? I liked to listen to him, too. Maybe when I grow up, my voice will be like Chuck Thompson's. You know what, it didn't work out that way.

But still, playing the game is what it's all about. So you play legion ball and you're fortunate enough to play in high school for John Keegan and at Illinois Wesleyan University, baseball for Jack Horenberger and football for Don Larson. And you play in summer leagues and then you're lucky enough to get to broadcast some high school and college basketball during your last three years in college. Getting the opportunity to work with two talented professionals like Don Munson and Don Newberg at WJBC Radio while still in college, great on-the-job training, priceless, invaluable.

And two years later, with a big assist from Jack Brickhouse, you are hired. Suddenly you're a big league announcer. How in the world did that happen so fast? And when you start out, you're working with one of the best, Buddy Blattner, and what a great teacher he was. More lessons and now you learn to do your homework.

There came a point during my second year, 1970, when I thought my broadcasting career had come to a screeching halt. Now, those of you who listen to big league games, you'll know that every once in a while we have commercial drop-ins, eight or 10 seconds, and you just in between pitches or between batters drop in a little one-liner. One of our sponsors was a company in Kansas City that made snack foods, potato chips, party nuts, pretzels. They were called Guy's Foods, owned by a nice, little 80-year-old man named Guy Caldwell. We are in Milwaukee, we are coming up on the Fourth of July weekend holiday. So I remember the producer handed me a little card that said "Guy's Foods," so I was supposed to think of a one-liner that would be timely and appropriate and so I said in a burst of brilliance, "For those of you planning a party, make sure you take along plenty of those good Guy's potato chips." It was kind of a slow game, and I think Al Fitzmorris, he was about to throw another pitch, and I thought, *You know what, that was pretty good. They are a good sponsor so give it another shot.* And the next line out of my mouth was, "And fans, while you're in the store, be sure and grab Guy's nuts," at which point I thought my budding broadcast career was over and go back to school and who knows what. You know what, I survived, Guy's Foods survived, and here we are 39 years later.

And so many people to thank and remember. My father, George, who was an All-American second baseman at Illinois State University and he gave his four sons an awareness and appreciation of the fun and the beauty of the game of baseball. He always encouraged us to play hard, play smart, play well, and have fun. The support of a mother, Eileen. She never failed to keep dinner warm after a long game or a practice. Three younger brothers, Steve, Doug, Mike, all good athletes, I think, aren't you? All very competitive who, by the way, I dominated in the backyard until all three got bigger, faster, and better.

I've had three main broadcasting partners in 39 years, my first partner, the original voice of the Royals, the very talented Buddy Blattner, my coach, my mentor, so helpful, so knowledgeable, and so courageous to hire a young guy just out of college with very little broadcasting experience. I couldn't do it without him. Fred White, my partner for 25 years, two guys from central Illinois who had the opportunity to broadcast the most exciting and significant games in Royals history. And now Ryan Lefebvre. We share similar backgrounds, a delight to work with, Ryan has a bright future. He will go a long way in the business. And only two producer/engineers in 39 years, that's pretty remarkable, the extremely capable Ed Shepherd and Don Free.

I find it hard to imagine any baseball announcer lucky enough to work for two better team owners, Ewing Kauffman and family and David Glass and family. Remarkable people, wanting only the best for the baseball fans of Kansas City, they are dedicated to that goal, passionate to that end, competing against the big-market advantages, and all the while staying true to their Midwestern values and beliefs. Royals fans are, have been, and will be blessed to have them. David and Ruth Glass, Dan and Penny Glass are here. Thanks for everything.

The Royals have had a succession of excellent general managers. One of them is here today, John Schuerholz from Baltimore. John joined the Oriole organization, and then in 1969, John and I both went to work for the Royals. John, thanks for being here. And I thank so much the friends here from all over the country, great friends from childhood, high school, college, and beyond. I'm thrilled and honored that they are here to share in this.

Kansas City has been honored previously here in Cooperstown, and I'm so proud to be standing here. Ernie Harwell, who stood here in 1984 with our great writer Joe McGuff, who won the Spink Award. (In) 1999 George Brett, the first Royals player to go into the Hall of Fame. George, thanks for being here. And just last year, my good friend, Buck O'Neil, and Buck stood right here. And you know what, folks? If Buck was sitting behind me this afternoon on the platform, I think right about now you'd hear, "Oh, yeah, that's right." Buck, we do miss him.

As a baseball broadcaster, I often think about our listeners and I often think about our fans. But, wait, aren't they one and the same? Think back to when you were a child, when you really started to follow this great game of baseball, and I'm curious, were you a fan who became a listener, or were you a listener who became a fan? Either way, I now think of you all as friends, and your hospitality really astounds me. You invited my voice into your homes, into your families, into your lives. I know because many of you have told me, in your kitchen, on your patio, in your car, your office, your family room, your basement, you've allowed my voice to ricochet around your garage, fishing boat. You've taken me on picnics and camping trips, but the essence of what a baseball broadcaster does is so well defined in a letter I received a few years ago from a lady out in Kansas, and bear with me because I've got a tough time getting through this letter.

"Dear Denny, I have loved baseball my whole life. I played softball as a young girl. I have listened to you since the Royals started in 1969. I am 93. I can't do the things I used to do. I can't see very well any more, but that's okay because I have my radio. So you are my eyes at the ballpark. I don't have to see because you create the picture in my mind with your words. Through your eyes and your words, I feel like I'm sitting at the ballpark watching the game. Listening to the Royals is the highlight of my day. It gives me something to look forward to, so keep up the good work. Sincerely, Margaret Jenkins."

Margaret, I hope you're still listening because it's folks like you that inspire us to do what we do.

Fans, listeners, friends, my profound thanks to all of you for loving the greatest game in the greatest nation on the face of the earth. Thank you.

CHAPTER 2
ROYAL RENAISSANCE

The great franchise the Kauffmans built went through tough times in the 1990s and early part of this century, but having culminated the 2015 season with a World Series title, the Royals are now once again the toast of Major League Baseball. From the last pitch of that World Series in New York to the parade, those few days included some of the coolest moments I've ever experienced. We had three jets full of people and occupied parts of three hotels in New York. According to the itinerary before the series started, if there was a fifth game on Sunday, we were supposed to leave for Kansas City after the game that night. So I checked out of the hotel and boarded the bus to the stadium around 1:00 PM. When I got on the bus, I was told that the Royals decided to spend the night, win or lose, so we were going to a new hotel.

We headed to Citi Field, the Royals won in dramatic fashion, and we stayed on the field doing interviews until the Mets ungraciously kicked us out by turning off the lights. (That may not seem like a big deal, or maybe our organization is unique. Either way, when San Francisco beat us at Kauffman Stadium in Game 7 in 2014, the Royals let the Giants celebrate at the stadium as long as they wanted to, even lighting the fountains orange for them.) We were at Citi Field until about 2:00 on Monday morning.

We then went to the New York Palace Hotel and had a huge celebration in the lobby and bar of the hotel. The World Series trophy was there, so anyone who wanted to could get a picture with it. We partied until about 5:30 in the morning when one of the hotel managers came over and said, "We're out of food and drink and we have to get ready for breakfast." Though we shut the party down, many of the celebrations continued until we left on the bus around 10.

The team had nine buses leaving at three different times. When we got to the airport, we went through security and went to one of the planes sitting on the tarmac. The media was on the plane with the players and their families. But when I boarded, there were no players to be found.

We kept waiting and waiting. I was in the first row of the plane, near George Brett and Ned Yost, when Jeff Davenport, the team's traveling secretary, got on and told us why we were delayed. Evidently, Johnny Cueto hadn't made it back to the hotel when it was time to leave, so he told his buddy to park his car in front of the players' bus so it wouldn't leave. If this was after a World Series loss, people might've cared. Under the circumstances I don't think too many people were concerned that the players were late.

When we arrived at KCI, we were taken to a private part of the airport. Somehow fans heard because there were hundreds of people there with signs and banners welcoming home the 2015 World Series champions. Once we got on the buses, we had a police escort to Kauffman Stadium, but throughout the entire ride, people were standing on the roadways and on the bridges, cheering for us. It was unbelievable. Of course, when we got to the stadium, there were hundreds of people waiting. That was just the start of the fanfare. There was going to be a little parade the next day.

In 2014 FOX Sports Kansas City let us know that if the Royals beat San Francisco and there was a parade, we'd cover it. If there wasn't a parade, there'd be a welcome back celebration for the players at Kauffman Stadium, and we'd cover that. Of course, the Royals lost, but about 15,000 people showed up at the stadium that day to show their appreciation. It seemed like the city couldn't get enough of the Royals.

After the 2015 World Series victory, this time we were going to be covering the parade. We were broadcasting it with FOX 4, the local affiliate. Since we'd never broadcast a parade, we were told to be at Union Station by 9:00 AM to go over the broadcast rundown. Normally, it would be a 25-minute drive or so from my house downtown. So, to be on the safe side and anticipating a crowd, I left at 7:50. As I got off at The Paseo and Bruce Watkins, all I could see were cars. And I wasn't even close to Union Station yet! I started following some other cars, literally driving

About 800,000 fans came out to celebrate our 2015 World Series title.
(Jeff Montgomery)

on sidewalks at times until we weren't going any farther, so I stopped and parked. Thankfully it was a beautiful day because the GPS on my phone said I was 63 minutes away. I was going to make a call to let the producers know I'd be late, but I couldn't get cell service because of all the people. I walked so fast that I got there in 50 minutes. As soon as I got there, I took my coat and tie off because I was sweating like crazy. When I finally got past Crown Center and over to Union Station, I realized the magnitude of this parade. It was a phenomenal sight. Hundreds of thousands of people were there, including kids, who'd gotten out of school around the city, and they were hanging from trees or sitting on dad's shoulders.

The plan was for us to get interviews with the players for about 20 minutes once they started arriving at Union Station. It was Rex Hudler,

Joel Goldberg, and me hosting from our temporary set, which was less than 100 feet from the stage. Once the parade got going, my job was to go into the private area and do one-on-one interviews with the players and coaches. I came to find out that people had been staking their spots for hours near the stage, so getting through the crowd was proving impossible. Squeezing through a brick wall would be easier. Finally, a police officer recognized me, and when I told him what I was trying to do, he helped me break through the sea of blue. We got set up in time to do the interviews and have a fun show. It's impossible to describe the amount of energy around downtown for that parade. I have a panoramic photo of the crowd hanging behind my desk. Every time I look at it, it gives me enduring memories of a long, incredible day.

After the Royals won the World Series, as is customary, the team was going to get a chance to meet with the president at the White House. When the Royals won in 1985, they went a few days later to meet with president Ronald Reagan. These days, for various scheduling reasons, teams typically don't visit the White House as soon. The Royals' trip was scheduled for an off day in 2016. I assumed it would be players, coaches, key front-office personnel, and that'd be about it. I was floored when my wife, Tina, and I received a nice invitation from team president Dan Glass.

The trip was more than we could've imagined. We did more in 24 hours than most people do in a lifetime. We left after a day game, took a chartered flight, and landed late that evening in Washington, D.C. The next morning we went to the White House.

We encountered a ton of security before walking through the doors, but once we got into the White House itself, it was pretty wide open. I thought someone would be directing us or telling us where we could and couldn't go, but that wasn't the case. We were able to roam from room to room in the section that was open and look at all of the displays. There were assistants in each room to give us history about the room or purpose for it, but they weren't guiding us or keeping us out. They were there to answer questions.

Players and staff, who were going to be on stage with president Barack Obama, were in a different area getting prepped for the ceremony while their wives, the media, and the rest of the traveling party not on stage were enjoying the opportunity to ask questions and see as much as we could. About 30 minutes or so before the ceremony was scheduled to start, we all went to our reserved seats in the East Room. There were a lot of politicians from this area in attendance, but it was great to see senator Bob Dole. A few minutes after we sat down, a couple hundred more people, who either requested to be there or were invited by their congressman or whomever, came in and sat down in the empty seats. A lot of Royals fans made the trip. In all, there were probably 300 people in there. Once everyone was seated, the players and front-office staff filed in. And then the president arrived and welcomed everyone.

BARACK OBAMA TRANSCRIPT

President Obama: Thank you! Everybody, have a seat. Have a seat. Welcome to the White House everybody. Let's give it up for the World Series champions, the Kansas City Royals! I know many of you had been waiting a long time to hear this, so I'll say it again—the World Series champion Kansas City Royals!

As you can tell, we've got quite a few Royals fans in the house, including some members of Congress. I see some members of my Cabinet, as well as former Cabinet members. We're also proud to be joined by a true American patriot, a World War II veteran, and one of the finest public servants America has ever known, senator Bob Dole.

I also want to recognize the Kansas City mayors from both sides of the border—Sly James. There he is. And Mark Holland. More importantly, Mark's son, Luke. Shortstop on—what's the name of your team?

Luke Holland: The Braves.

Obama: The Braves? Not the Atlanta Braves, just want to be clear. But he's a shortstop. Skip, you may want to check out what he's got.

We're proud to have Royals owner David Glass and team president Dan Glass here. Give them a big round of applause. We've got general manager Dayton Moore here. Two of the greatest Royals of all time—George Brett and Frank White. And the winningest manager in Royals history—give it up for Ned Yost!

Now, I'm not sure if anybody is aware of this, but my press secretary happens to be a Royals fan. Where's Josh? There he is right in the front row. If you asked Josh to choose the best day of his life, I'm pretty sure he'd say his wedding day and the birth of his son. But this is close. It's really close. I notice he has his son here, training him—even though he's more interested right now in sucking his thumb (than learning) to be a proper Royals fan.

And let's face it, it's been a long road for Royals fans. There were some dark years, some tough decades. But that started to change when Dayton came to town in 2006. He coupled some of baseball's sharpest analytics minds with Ned's managerial style, which has produced a lot of wins, not to mention his own Twitter hashtag—#Yosted. All of which has combined to create one of the grittiest, most complete teams we've seen in a long time.

You've got an offense led by homegrown guys like Alex "Gordo" Gordon and Mike "Moose" Moustakas, Eric "Hoz" Hosmer, World (Series) MVP Salvador "Salvy" Perez. These guys are all great players. Can I say, though, the nicknames aren't that creative. It's like, Barack "Barack" Obama. You know? I mean, listen to this—Hoz, Moose, Gordo. We're going to have to work on these.

Also lights-out bullpen with relievers like Wade Davis and Kelvin

Herrera. You got a speedy, athletic defense led by Alcides Escobar and Lorenzo Cain, who couldn't make it today.

Audience: Aww...

Obama: Aww...

At the plate, you've got guys who hardly ever strike out. They've been called "basically the best contact team ever." So fast, once around base, they're able to squeeze out extra runs, because as— I love this quote—as Jarrod Dyson puts it, "that's what speed do." That's what speed do. That was a good quote. That's what speed do.

And then somehow they find the time still to sneak Fetty Wap references into their press conferences. Josh, you haven't done that, have you?

Josh Earnest: No, I have not.

Obama: Good, okay.

So you can see why Royals fans love this team so much. And I mean *love* this team—800,000 at a parade. Last year, fans swamped the All-Star balloting process to the point that it looked like the entire starting lineup was going to be Royals. And as a Chicago guy, I appreciate that. Vote early, vote often. So that was good.

So, together, you guys have been on quite a ride. For two seasons, every playoff game seems like it's been a white-knuckle game. Wild comeback against the A's two years ago. The rally in Game 7 against the Giants that came up 90 feet short. Last year, coming back from the Astros. Down three against the Blue Jays. Down in each of their World Series wins against the Mets. In all, they have had eight comeback wins in the playoffs—which is a major league record.

And that includes Game 5 of the World Series—a ninth-inning comeback capped by Hoz's gutsy dash home on an infield grounder. And then in the 12th, in his first at-bat of last year's postseason, Christian Colon clinched the series with a pinch-hit, go-ahead single that opened up the floodgates.

Now, I think Christian's play—somebody who hadn't been used a lot, then suddenly coming up big when the moment arrived for him—that's exactly the "keep the line moving" mentality that's defined this team. Guys aren't in it for themselves; they're in it for each other, both on and off the diamond.

This spring the Royals broke ground on their Urban Youth Academy in Kansas City—a place for young people to not only steer clear of drugs and gangs, but to also learn skills that can lead to a better future. And that means not just playing baseball but learning about advanced stats and broadcasting and sports-writing and having access to tutoring and internships, college prep, financial literacy courses. This is in keeping with the kind of efforts that we've been promoting with My Brother's Keeper. And I just to want recognize Royals ownership as well as players—Gordo, Hoz, Salvy, Moose, Chris Young—who donated millions of dollars toward supporting Kansas City's young people. They deserve a big round of applause for that.

And what's great is the academy is built right next to the Negro League Museum—so you can see the link between Jackie Robinson and Satchel Paige, to Frank White and to George Brett, to Salvador Perez and Alex Gordon, and the next generation of Kansas City baseball stars. And you see that continuity and understand how central this game is to America.

So I want to thank this group for not only writing the current chapter, but hopefully writing the next chapter of our national pastime, the great game of baseball.

Give it up one last time for the world champs, Kansas City Royals!

Visiting the White House and meeting President Obama is an experience I will never forget. *(Jeff Montgomery)*

It was a very excitable crowd, at one point even breaking into a "Let's Go Royals!" chant. It was such an honor to be able to enjoy it. When the president was done, we went to a reception area and then got on buses and headed to the airport. We were in the air about an hour or so after the president finished.

Regardless of your political affiliation, being that close to our nation's president and being in a building with such history as the White House is incredible. It was another remarkable moment in this Royal renaissance.

Much has been written about the Royals of recent years. Their renaissance—if you will—has been covered extensively in other books, including one from the architect, Dayton Moore. Having covered the club in recent years, though, I'm often asked about some of the main moments and, especially, the pitching. But what we've seen with back-to-back World Series appearances, including the 2015 championship, starts at the top, and it began in the middle of the 2006 season.

The first time I ever heard Dayton Moore speak was at his introductory press conference in June 2006. He had been hired from the Atlanta Braves, where he worked under our former general manager, John Schuerholz. Dayton was talking about how they had a plan to get the franchise back to the top, and, although the fans weren't going to like this, it was going to be an eight to 10-year process to get where they needed to be. They were going to do it by building the farm system with an emphasis on arms, stockpiling arms at every level and they were going to build from there. The phrase he used that day and often since: "Pitching is the currency of baseball."

Shortly after that the Royals alumni was asked to meet with Dayton. He expressed his need to have the alumni help in any way they could. At that time the alumni were more attractive than the current roster. He said how the alumni could be a tremendous asset to what he wanted to do. He was very straightforward and very honest about his objective and how he was going to do it. All of the former players bought in that day. It's similar to what he's been able to do with the Glass family. Dayton earned our trust and respect from what he did prior to coming to Kansas City and what he could do if given the right chance.

He was able to make the Royals alumni group feel as though we were going to have a part in the turnaround of the organization. Today, there are several alums in the Royals organization, particularly as coaches at the various minor league levels. He's used that asset as a productive tool. He also recognized the importance of the heritage of the organization and its players. He made sure that history is on display in places where the players see it: the clubhouses and spring training facility. We have the Royals Alumni Guest Instructor Program where every spring there are a handful of Royals alums who participate in spring training at the minor league level. Ronnie Richardson coordinates it. They have us on the field with the minor league guys for a week. We help them, talk to them, have small group meetings with them. It works on two levels, allowing us to get to know future Royals and also to get the young players to understand more about the history of the organization.

During that first discussion with the alumni, Dayton identified specific scouts, coaches, and front-office personnel from around baseball that he had his sights set on bringing to Kansas City. He went through names and positions of very highly qualified baseball people whom he wanted to have part of the process. There were a lot of impressive names on the list who ultimately were involved in building here. It was obvious that not only did he have an overall plan of turning around this organization that had experienced 100-loss seasons and was involved in Major League Baseball's contraction talks, but he also had a specific plan of attack. That's impressive to see from someone who had never been a general manager.

In his first few years in Kansas City, Dayton and I lived in the same neighborhood, and we both ran quite a bit. Occasionally, we'd pass each other and start running together. From the first time we did that, it was obvious he was very open-minded about how he and the organization could get better. He's asked me and other alums a lot, "What do you see in our club right now?" He wants to get a feel from outside sources what the Royals can do to improve.

Dayton took a lot of criticism from the media and fans during most of his time from 2006 until 2014, but he remained positive and focused on his plan. So when the Royals won the World Series, he was the person I was happiest for—more than any individual—because of what he poured into it and everything he had to overcome. I'm happy for everyone from the fans up to the Glass family, but if I had to pick one guy, it'd be Dayton.

I remember driving back to the WHB offices after a Royals day game in mid-May 2010 and hearing on the radio that Dayton had relieved Trey Hillman of his duties as manager of the Royals after a 12–23 start. When I arrived at the 810 studios, I was asked to go on the air with

Kevin Kietzman and Danny Clinkscale to discuss the managerial situation. As is the norm when a manager is let go, there are lots of emotions involved, and players comment that it was not the manager's fault and that they wish they had performed better so their manager's fate would have been better.

It was very interesting to learn that Hillman had been notified of his firing the day before but asked Dayton to give him one more game so that he could possibly go out a winner, which he did when Zack Greinke beat the Cleveland Indians 6–4 on May 13, giving Zack his first win of 2010.

When Dayton announced that Ned Yost was going to take over for Hillman, the opinions on the hiring ranged about as much as could be expected. Those who remembered Ned's last year as skipper with the Milwaukee Brewers couldn't believe he was getting another shot to manage in the big leagues. Those who remembered him as a coach for several years under Bobby Cox in Atlanta thought he was the perfect manager for the Royals.

The common thread between Milwaukee, Atlanta, and Kansas City was that all three organizations that had floundered near the bottom for years and needed someone to guide them through rebuilding to become contenders. The Braves accomplished this and more for a decade and a half and became a perennial playoff team. Ned had witnessed much of that. Though not as successful as the Braves when measured by playoff appearances, the Brewers accomplished the rebuilding portion of the task. And they developed an excellent crop of quality major league players.

The Royals were just a few years into the Dayton Moore era but were at a crucial point in development as some of the amateur talent that Moore and company had drafted were knocking on the door of the major leagues. The right manager was critical in providing the environment for the finishing touches to be added.

The second half of the 2014 season and the incredible October the Royals experienced confirmed to me that Ned was the right manager to guide the current group of players through some difficult waters. His commitment to his roster and the way he has consistently backed his players paid off in a large way as the club closed in on its first World Series appearance since 1985.

Although there were several who wanted to run Ned out of Kansas City when he replaced James Shields with Yordano Ventura during the wild-card game against the Oakland A's (see the social media hashtag #Yosted), it very well may have been his commitment to his troops that allowed them to overcome enormous odds and win that game.

For all of the haters, though, Dayton stuck with Ned, and Ned continued to be a positive force who believes in his players. And on June 18, 2015, Ned did something no one expected when he surpassed Whitey Herzog as the winningest manager in Royals history. Ned picked up win No. 411 at home against, of all teams, the Brewers. Coincidentally, it was one of Ned's former Milwaukee players, Alcides Escobar, who propelled the Royals to the 3–2 victory with three hits and two runs. It's easy to see now that Yost was the right man for the job.

Before Dayton and Ned came to Kansas City, there was Zack. Early in his career, WHB was the rights holder for the Royals games. I was in the station's suite during a game one night, along with Bret Saberhagen and George Brett. We were talking about this kid who was going to start the next game. There were so many comparisons between Greinke and Saberhagen. When Sabes came up, he'd stayed with Mark Gubicza at George's house. Coincidentally, Greinke was staying at George's when he first came up.

We'd arranged dinner at Plaza III with George, Sabes, a couple of George's friends, and Zack. During dinner we're talking about things that Zack liked to do outside of baseball and what he liked about the game. Somewhat quietly he said, "I'm not so sure I shouldn't have been a shortstop because starting pitching is boring." Overall, though, it was a good and enlightening conversation. At the time Plaza III was a radio sponsor on WHB, and when a player did an interview, he'd get a Plaza III certificate. When the check came, Zack pulled out his certificate for his meal. George said, "No, put that away. I got it."

"No, use it," Zack said, "I'll never come back to this place."

"Why not?"

"It's too expensive."

"Where do you like to eat?"

"Chipotle."

* * *

For most of the past two decades, late summer meant that most Kansas City sports fans had shifted their focus to Chiefs training camp and optimism for an exciting football season on the horizon. For college football fans, it meant that Saturday afternoons full of college spirit were just around the corner.

In 2013, however, that started to change. Royals fans had reason to take a look at the Major League Baseball standings on a daily basis. The hopes of postseason baseball were not in immediate grasp for the boys, but at least their play since the All-Star break put them in position to have a real chance of playing meaningful baseball late into the season.

One could cite many games or plays in the second half that provided optimism for the Royals. More than anything, a nine-game winning streak did. That was a turning point in the season. To win nine in a row, there are several things that need to go right. You need to miss a few opponents' aces, you need to beat a few staff aces, and you need to beat teams that have essentially given up on the season. And the Royals did all of that.

For a team like the Royals that had lost for so long, it is very difficult to change their losing ways because everyone expects the worst to happen at some point. In 2012 we saw it in April when they lost 12 straight games. We saw it again in the early part of 2013, when they went 8–20 in May and lost five straight before the All-Star break.

Fortunately, that group had overcome some pretty big hurdles, but the focus they showed was different than recent years and was an important factor as they moved forward. It has often been said that before a team can make it to the top it has to learn how to win. The Royals started to do that in 2013, and it carried over for the next two seasons.

There have been a lot of mentions in recent years about the 2014 team meeting with Raul Ibanez. There's good reason for talking about Raul. That's when we started to see the Royals' formation of a team approach to playing baseball. At the All-Star break in 2014, which was supposed to be their year, they were just so-so. In a press conference around that time, Ned was talking about how the team proved in '13 that it's a good second-half team. "We'll be just fine," Ned said.

Then we went to Boston and got swept and lost a game in Chicago. I wondered where these second-half guys had gone. When we arrived in Chicago, I saw Dayton Moore in the hotel. He didn't travel a lot so he was there for a reason. Joel Goldberg and I had him on the pregame show before the second game in Chicago, and I asked him on the air, "Where does Ned stand?" Dayton gave a detailed description of their confidence in Ned and how Dayton was in Chicago for a vote of confidence. How often do we hear that in all sports right before a guy gets fired? That's when Ibanez had the team meeting. That led to a different approach for the team's style of play. Guys checked their egos and started playing for the names on the front of their jerseys instead of the back. And Ned was right; they were a good second-half team. Ironically, they clinched a wild-card spot in Chicago at the end of the season. That was an incredible celebration and deserving because of how long it'd been since the last celebration. It was a lot of fun.

The Bullpen

Perhaps this is a little bias coming out, but the most impressive part of the Royals in the last several years is the bullpen. Guys get hurt, and others step up. They redefine themselves. In whatever combination of players it has featured, the bullpen has been the stabilizing force for this recent run of success.

Each player has to perform to his own strength. If a guy has a tremendous fastball, he needs to use it. Sometimes guys get better when they learn a new pitch. Kelvin Herrera, for instance, became a better pitcher after he learned to throw the slider. He wasn't just a hard thrower then. A pitcher has to be himself and use those key assets to the fullest. It's taken some trial and error to find the right combination and to make sure skills match up with the requirements of being in the bullpen.

Danny Duffy started trusting his fastball. He condensed his curve and slider into more of a slurve and he's using a power breaking ball. Originally, he was okay as a starter, moved to the bullpen, and was effective as a reliever. He started 2016 in the bullpen and used that as a chance to either build or regain confidence needed in his fastball. Ned Yost was looking for a fifth starter once the season got going, and suddenly Danny became an option. I wasn't convinced it was a good move because he had been so successful in the bullpen, but he went out there and dealt. Some of his early starts in '16 were a bit ugly because he wasn't ready to throw 110 pitches. Now I don't know that there's anyone I'd want starting a pivotal game more than Duffy. He was at a point in his mind that it was time to put up or shut up. He's now doing what he felt he should've done when he came up in 2011. On top of that, Danny is a tremendous, unselfish person who wants to be the best asset he can be for his team.

After struggling to find a closer during their first few American League West titles, the Royals went from Dan Quisenberry to me for a span of about 15 years. Then they had a revolving door for a few years until Joakim Soria came on. I remember numerous years in September when sportswriters would call me about my single-season saves record being broken. I'd tell them, "It's not my record; it's Quiz's record." Soria, during his first stint with the Royals from 2007 to 2011, became that good. If the team would've won more games, Soria would've broken Quiz's record.

The Soria we saw in 2016 was not the same consistent one we saw early in his career. Father Time is undefeated, and he looked to be catching up with Soria. That happened to me late in my career, too. I wasn't as good early in the season, but I finished better. After I was probably 32 or 33 years old (28-32 is the prime), I got by more on experience. Older pitchers are better later in the season; younger guys wear down in the second half, and it evens out the talent and ability.

Greg Holland and Wade Davis are the two relievers who had the most unhittable stuff in Royals history. And they did it with two different styles. Holland is the only person I remember having a Kevin Appier-like slider because it had more bottom-out life. Holland is very similar to Ape in terms of style. Holland got to a point when he probably tried to hit bats more than Ape did, but they would miss bats with very similar stuff.

After tying the Royals' single-season saves record with his 45th save of the year in September 2013 against the Seattle Mariners, Holland put himself in a position to eclipse the record Quisenberry established 30 years ago. In terms of saves, Holland put together what many feel is the greatest single season by any Royals reliever in team history. That year Holland was recognized as an All-Star for the first time in his career for his dominance of the American League. He went on to save 46 games in 2014.

None of that would have been possible without Holland's drive and determination. That drive is what allowed him to overcome enormous odds to even have the opportunity to play college baseball. Holland was not recruited to play college baseball out of McDowell High School

I really respect the drive and determination of Greg Holland, who saved a Royals-record 47 games in 2013. *(Kansas City Royals)*

in Marion, North Carolina, but he was so determined to play that he walked on at Western Carolina University. He eventually persevered and was first team All-Southern Conference as a junior.

After Holland's junior year, the Royals made him their 10th round draft choice in 2007. They promoted him to the big leagues in 2010, which made him the first draft pick from Dayton Moore's regime to make it to the majors. Still, he was never a player who everyone looked at and could say with certainty that he would achieve the level of success that he has had. I could pull for him easily because I could see some of myself in him. We both played at mid-level schools in the Southern Conference (Marshall for me) and we were both undersized pitchers who weren't projected to be major league pitchers.

He struggled with command early, as many pitchers do. Holland was not a model of consistency during his 15-game debut in 2010, but he continued to work to be better. Pitchers doubt themselves when they're first called up until they enjoy some success and lose the fear of hitting bats. He developed trust in his defense, but he had great ability to miss bats. Holland became a pitcher who could do that with a large amount of consistency. It was exciting for me to see him establish himself as a major league pitcher.

I really admired and learned a lot in 2015 about a major characteristic of Holland: he's a bulldog. When I saw him early in the season, he had a neoprene sleeve around his elbow, which gave me a sense that something was wrong. We didn't talk about it at all on the air, but I mentioned to some of the broadcast crew that because of the wrap around his elbow that he wore during batting practice and in the clubhouse I didn't think he was 100 percent. There'd been no public talk about any type of injury or setback, but when I saw that sleeve, it was an alarm that told me something wasn't quite right. As the season went on, a few guys on the broadcast crew told me that I might be right. Neither Holland nor the club disclosed anything, but speaking with Dayton around the midpoint of the season, he said they wanted to keep their eye on him because they didn't know how much more he could go out there.

Holland didn't want the Royals to shut him down. He was willing to pitch, even though, as we found out later, there was a significant amount of damage to his elbow. He pitched into September and saved 32 games in 2015 before eventually having Tommy John surgery. He was instrumental in the Royals' success that season. Even though he was watching the postseason celebrations from the sidelines, he was a big reason they were there. A lot of guys want to be 100 percent before they take the mound, but Holland wanted to be out there and still achieved a high level of success without being 100 percent. It takes a special player to climb the mound and help his team when he's not at full strength.

Now, not only is Holland a tremendous talent to watch, but he has also been a great story of the little guy who has persevered and transitioned into one of the best at what he does and he is so easy to pull for because of all he has endured to obtain his success.

When other broadcasters ask me what makes Wade so good, I say it's his ability to throw his cut fastball, especially to left-handed hitters. It gets that cutting action at the end and shaves the corner of the plate. Hitters give up on it. He has pinpoint control with it. He gets so many called strikes because the hitter thinks it's going to be a ball, but it has incredible movement in the last five feet. His command of that pitch, coupled with an overhand curveball and a four-seam fastball, make him one of the most difficult guys to hit. The best hitters in the world have trouble making contact, let alone getting hits.

In 2014 Luke Hochevar was going to be the set-up man for Greg, but Hoch hurt his elbow in spring training. That opened the door for Wade. What did he do? He turned in one of the most impressive and dominating seasons we'll ever see. Wade didn't allow a run for 20 appearances and didn't give up an extra-base hit for 43 appearances. He ended with a 1.00 ERA in 71 games. Then, in 2015, Holland's injured elbow opened the door for Davis to be the closer. What did he do? He recorded a 0.94 ERA in 69 outings.

We saw Davis go through stretches, even in 2015, when he wasn't as dominant, but he got the job done. He had to work to get through some innings and he had stretches of a dead arm, but he got back and came back with that pinpoint control.

One Davis moment I won't forget is his performance in Game 6 of the 2015 American League Championship Series against the Toronto Blue Jays. With the Royals leading 3–1, Ryan Madson came in and gave up a two-run home run to Jose Bautista in the eighth. Davis came in and bailed out Madson. Then a 45-minute rain delay hit. That's a long time for a pitcher to have to wait, especially when the Royals were due to bat right after the delay before Wade came back out. The Royals took the lead in the bottom of the eighth after the delay, and then Wade took the mound for the ninth. Toronto put two in scoring position before Wade closed it out against Josh Donaldson, the American League MVP. It looked like Toronto might have a Royals-type comeback, but Wade squashed it. As stressful as this can be for some people, I always felt, that as a closer, sometimes getting a couple base runners on will make you elevate your game. Fear of failure was a huge motivating factor for me. That made me a better athlete, knowing that my manager, pitching coach, teammates, fans, and organization trusted me to be shaking hands at the end of the night. When I let them down, it was tough. Closers have to be willing to gamble at times. Maybe a change-up isn't the out pitch, but if the situation calls for it, you throw it. Wade seems to come up with those pitches at just the right time.

Wade's the best in the business at what he does. One of the keys is that he doesn't get too high or too low. The majority of dominant closers are like that. Look at Mariano Rivera. You wouldn't know if he struck out the side or gave up a grand slam. My job as a closer was to be shaking

Wade Davis embraces catcher Drew Butera after recording the final out in Game 5 to win the 2015 World Series. *(Kansas City Royals)*

hands after the game. That meant I finished the game out and my team won. Basically, I wanted to be a professional handshaker.

Of late, the Royals have become bound and determined to be the team shaking hands at the end of the game. Something magical has happened with this team that we rarely see: it doesn't matter what type of deficit these Royals are facing. They feel they can come back. Since 2014 it's in their DNA as a team that there are 27 outs, and they're going to play all 27 as hard as they can. Even after going to the World Series in

2014 and winning it in '15, we haven't seen a team that is content with just getting there. It's become ingrained in these Royals that they need to keep fighting.

It's hard to tell with this group of players if they're in first or last. When I was playing, it was tough after a loss. Sitting on the bus after a loss is very quiet. There's not a lot of chatter or happiness. But these guys enjoy each other—win, lose, or draw. That's not to say they're happy or content with losing; this team just shares a closeness I've never been around in professional baseball. A lot of it is the result of their success. They're confident enough that they've adopted this mantra following a loss: hey, you beat us tonight, but we'll beat you tomorrow.

We've seen some incredible comebacks in recent years. The ones that stand out most to me are the ones in postseason elimination games, such as Game 4 of the 2015 American League Division Series against Houston, when we scored seven runs in the last two innings and beat the Astros 9–6 and brought the series back to Kansas City for the clinching game. Even in the final two World Series games against the New York Mets, the Royals overcame late deficits.

I think this "we're playing 27 outs" mentality goes back to the 2014 wild-card game against the Oakland A's. So many things went on in that game, but that was the one that taught them how to win those games that seemingly are all but over. It created a mind-set for this group of players, an understanding that it's not over until the 27th out is made.

James Shields, who was instrumental in the Royals turning the corner, started, and the Royals had a lead until the sixth inning. Ned Yost took out James and brought in Yordano Ventura, who immediately gave up a home run to Brandon Moss. That's when I thought it was over. *There were 40,000 people at Kauffman, and they waited 29 years for this?* The A's had a really good team, and they had their hired gun, Jon Lester, who'd had tremendous success against the Royals, on the mound. With a 7–3 lead in that situation, he looked unstoppable. When the Royals started to get that line moving in the eighth inning, though, it was incredible. We were going to be doing a postgame show, win or lose. I—all of us, really—went from one level of disappointment to a level of pandemonium in such a short amount of time.

After tying the game in the bottom of the ninth, the Royals won it in the 10th inning when Salvador Perez reached out and lined a two-out hit past Josh Donaldson, scoring Eric Hosmer from third. Once they won, I started to think it was destiny for them to win the World Series. I probably felt better about their chances of winning the World Series in '14 than I did in '15. The novelty of it was special as was the way to start off the American League playoffs 8–0 and get to the World Series. With the way the Royals were playing, the only person who could've beaten them in the World Series was San Francisco Giants pitcher Madison Bumgarner. When they had the momentum after the wild-card, it seemed like they wouldn't lose again.

My All-Time Royals Team

The following are the best players who were either my contemporaries or guys I've covered as a broadcaster. So that's why you won't see Royals greats like Amos Otis or Steve Busby on the list. One caveat to add: if I was torn between two players, I picked the guy who won championships here or elsewhere. Though I didn't experience the postseason as a player, having been involved as a broadcaster in recent years and seeing the intensity of every pitch and every hit and every catch, I've realized what a qualifier that is for a great player.

Catcher

Picking Salvador Perez was tough for me only because Mike Macfarlane and Brent Mayne were so great behind the plate for me. But they weren't Salvador Perez. I'll always remember when Ned Yost took over as manager in midseason 2010. Jason Kendall caught 118 games that year but blew out his shoulder in August. Reporters asked Ned who his new catcher was going to be. Ned, who'd been roving in the Royals' minor leagues before becoming manager, said, "There's a kid I'd bring up right now if they'd let me. He could catch here today, but he's not ready at the plate. His name is Salvador Perez." Salvy came up from Triple A Omaha and made his debut on August 10, 2011, and immediately made a splash. In that night's game, he picked off Casey Kotchman at first base in the bottom of the fourth inning and then he picked off Sam Fuld at third base in the eighth. (Those were the first two runners that a Kansas City catcher had picked off that season.) Oh, and Salvy got an RBI single and scored a run. He hit .331 the rest of that season after being called up.

First Base

Eric Hosmer does so many things well as a player, and his character in the clubhouse and off the field puts him over the top. I can't think of a first baseman who I'd rather have today. Miguel Cabrera hits for a better average, but Cabrera is a more offensive-minded player. Hosmer is more well-rounded. Let's not forget he helped the Royals clinch the 2015 World Series with his base-running ability. He also has an outstanding and accurate throwing arm. He's a Gold Glove first baseman for a reason.

Second Base

When I played with him, his best days were behind him, but Frank White has a statue of at Kauffman Stadium, and his No. 20 hangs on the side of the Royals Hall of Fame building. There's a reason for those things.

Shortstop

If you watch for a game or two, you may not understand the importance of Alcides Escobar. But watch him for the better part of a season and you'll see how good he is, game in and game out. He's on this list based on what he's done in the postseason, too. He was the 2015 American League Championship Series MVP.

Third Base

Okay, George Brett is clearly the best Royals player ever, so before jumping up and down about Brett not being my third baseman, remember that he didn't play third base when I was pitching. He'd made the transition to first base and designated hitter, and that's how I'm categorizing him on my list. So Mike Moustakas, who went from a player who was sent down to the minor leagues in 2014 only to have a turning point during that year's postseason, gets the nod here. In '15 he was a much better hitter and he could either use the opposite field or hit for power. He's also a great defensive player.

Outfielders

With these outfielders—Alex Gordon, Carlos Beltran, and Willie Wilson—we have great defenders and a lot of speed. I played with Beltran and Wilson. As far as Gordon, he has a gift to rise to the occasion whether it's with his glove or his arm or his bat. He is such a well-rounded player that he can beat the opponent in a variety of ways. He might make a diving catch that saves runs or he could hit a home run in the ninth inning off the opponent's dominant closer in Game 1 of the World Series. Alex and Beltran have similar skillsets, but being a switch-hitter gives Carlos a slight advantage. Note that it was very hard for me to leave out Lorenzo Cain. He has a lot of versatility defensively, so he can play all three outfield spots effortlessly. On offense he can hit big home runs when you need them.

Designated Hitter

One of the best hitters of all time, George Brett was a DH during my career, so it's a pretty easy choice here.

Starting Pitchers

A rotation of Bret Saberhagen, David Cone, Kevin Appier, Mark Gubicza, and Zack Greinke would be hard to beat.

Bullpen

Joakim Soria and I would handle the long relief, Wade Davis and Greg Holland would be the set-up guys, and the incomparable Dan Quisenberry would be the closer.

CHAPTER 3
FROM THE TOP DOWN

During my time playing for the Royals, the club had two general managers, four managers, and five different pitching coaches.

General Managers

To me, being traded from Cincinnati to Kansas City after the 1987 season was a huge sigh of relief because I didn't think I'd get a chance with the Reds. As a National League fan growing up and then as a player, I didn't know much about the Royals, so I assumed it would be a good situation, one that would allow me to start playing at the major league level immediately.

Within 20 minutes of arriving at spring training, I met a guy who appeared to be either a media type or someone from the front office. Sure enough, it was general manager John Schuerholz. He said, "Welcome to the Royals. We're glad to have you here. We've looked at your numbers as a starter and as a reliever. We really like you more as a reliever, so we're going to send you to Omaha to start the season and get some more experience as a reliever." My bubble burst immediately because I thought this was going to be my chance out of spring training. As it turned out, I had a good spring training and forced their hand a little. I pitched 20 games in Omaha in 1988 and got 13 saves.

From that moment in spring 1988 until October 1990, when John left Kansas City for the Atlanta Braves, John and I didn't interact much. During those first three seasons, I was trying to establish myself in the major leagues and get comfortable in a role, and John interacted more directly with the veteran players, such as George Brett, Willie Wilson, Bret Saberhagen, and so on. That's how things were in baseball at the time. John was a good general manager here, but he became a great GM with the Braves.

John was a brilliant baseball mind who built both the Royals and Braves into World Series champions. He deservedly was voted into the

Baseball Hall of Fame by a unanimous measure (all 16 of the Today's Game Era Committee) during the 2016 winter meetings.

At the time the Royals promoted him to general manager in 1981, the 40-year-old Schuerholz was the youngest general manager in baseball history. The Royals then made it to the postseason in 1984 before winning it all in 1985. A year after joining the Braves, they went from last place to first place en route to winning an amazing 14 straight division titles.

Though John did the leave Royals to go to the Braves, the move would go on to help Kansas City decades later in a kind of circular fashion. He hired Dayton Moore as an area scouting supervisor for the Braves in 1994. Dayton rose through the ranks under John and learned the trade under him while going from assistant director of scouting to assistant director of player development to director of international scouting to director of player personnel to assistant general manager before joining the Royals front office in 2006, where he, of course, revitalized the franchise.

I got to know Herk Robinson better than I did John because of our tenure together. When John left in the fall of 1990, the Royals turned to Herk, and he was the team's general manager through the rest of my career. I knew a lot about Herk. He had some Reds ties early in his career, so we had that in common.

Herk is sometimes criticized for not being a good general manager, but he had the difficult task of being Kansas City's GM during a transitional period with the organization and with Major League Baseball. It was a stage when the game was changing in terms of salary structure with many larger market owners opening their deep pockets and widening the salary gap between themselves and teams like Kansas City. Mr. Kauffman was willing to spend money to make the team better, but as with any good businessman, he wanted to limit his losses. Making Herk's job more difficult was that after Mr. K died he dealt with a board of directors overseeing the club. Going up to Mr. Kauffman and talking about a deal is different—and probably a little easier—than dealing with a board.

To say that I knew a lot about Herk isn't to say that we had a lot of interaction. One talk we had definitely stands out. I believe it was in 1994—after I was already established as a closer. It was difficult for me to be into every pitch for nine innings. Typically, I was a fan early, staying in the bullpen for the national anthem and the first inning or two and then I'd find a place to relax for a few innings. Oftentimes, that relaxation was going up the tunnel around the scoreboard and then washing or waxing my car. This particular night I decided it needed to be washed and waxed. It was really hot, so I took off my jersey, turned the game on the radio, and started washing and waxing my car. After a few minutes, a golf cart came down the tunnel. It was Herk on his way to talk to groundskeeper George Toma. Herk stopped and said, "Uh, Monty, do you mind me asking what you're doing?"

"I'm waxing my car."

"Isn't the game going on?"

"Yeah, it's 3–2 in the fourth inning."

"Do you do this often?"

"No, not really, just when my car needs to be waxed."

Herk gave me a blank stare for a moment and then said, "Well, I guess it works," and he drove down to visit with George.

Managers

Here's some trivia for you: I played for five managers during my major league career. All five were on their first managerial jobs. That includes Pete Rose in Cincinnati and then John Wathan, Hal McRae, Bob Boone, and Tony Muser in Kansas City.

I thought "Duke," John Wathan, was a great manager. He was being groomed at Triple A Omaha in 1987 and was probably rushed to Kansas City after Dick Howser died. Because he'd grown up in the organization, Duke had tremendous knowledge of Royals baseball in terms of both history and personnel. The difficult part for him was managing his former teammates. At some point I felt there was an awareness that it was going to be difficult for Duke because of those relationships from his playing days. Those guys didn't take advantage of that, but there definitely was less of an intimidation factor because of the friendships. Players have to be respectful of and intimidated by their manager enough that they're aware of possible repercussions for certain actions. That wasn't the case for some guys toward Duke. I felt like some of the players who were former teammates of Duke's could respond or comment to his managerial moves in a way that they probably wouldn't have with Dick Howser. It was a less-than-perfect situation.

His relationships with those players potentially were limiting factors in his managerial success, but there were benefits, too. He had been behind the plate catching Bret Saberhagen and Mark Gubicza, for instance, and he knew how to handle them better. Duke was excellent at handling players. He was always willing to do what he could do to better his team.

We were very successful in 1989, finishing the season with a 92–70 record, which created enormous expectations in 1990. John Schuerholz brought in pitchers Storm Davis and Mark Davis, who were seen as a couple of pieces to enhance our chances of winning the American League West. The only thing it did was create even bigger expectations. When we didn't live up to those expectations, especially early in the season, that was disappointing. We finished 75–86. Schuerholz left for Atlanta in October, and Herk Robinson became the general manager.

We started off the '91 season in slow fashion again, hovering at .500 after 16 games. But then we lost seven in a row and couldn't get a sustained winning streak going. We improved to 15–22 after beating the Seattle Mariners on May 21, but the next day Herk announced that Duke had been fired. I was at a luncheon the day they let Duke go. Team president Joe Burke was speaking at that luncheon, and he and I were guests at the head table. He told the crowd at the luncheon that they were going to make an announcement later that day that they were going to hire Hal McRae as the next manager. I about fell out of my chair. I had no idea they were going to fire Duke, but then we learned from the president of the club that I was going to be playing for McRae. I was stunned.

Even though this was Hal's first managerial job, he picked it up very quickly. I've heard stories about how he was a great teammate and leader and I could see why he had that reputation. I never had a chance to play with Mac, but there was a lot of respect for him. He was no-nonsense. He brought an aggressive, hard-nosed style of play from Cincinnati to Kansas City in the early 1970s, and that carried over to his managerial style. He was a great leader. Unlike Duke's situation, by the time Mac took over in '91, he had fewer former teammates as players. I don't think that would've mattered to him anyway. Hal was Hal. He wasn't going to deviate because this player or that player was a former teammate. The other players respected that, and I think that's one reason the Royals gave him the opportunity to manage.

The unique thing for Hal is that his son, Brian, who'd become a good friend of mine, was already established on the team. It was good that he was established, but B-Mac would've been an everyday player for nearly every team in the league at the time, so it's not like he was playing for the Royals because his dad was managing. Brian was similar to Hal. He was a hard-nosed player and a great teammate. He would try to run through a wall for you. The wall would win, but he'd try it if it meant helping a teammate. There was never an issue with Hal and Brian. Unless you knew there was a father-son relationship there, it probably wouldn't have been apparent that they were anything other than manager and player. They both handled it very professionally.

Hal took over on Friday, May 24, as we started a six-game road trip to Minnesota and Seattle. Gubie pitched the second game in the Twins

Though Hal McRae looks cool and composed here, he brought the aggressive and hard-nosed style from his playing days to his managerial role. *(Kansas City Royals)*

IF THESE WALLS COULD TALK: KANSAS CITY ROYALS

series, and it was one of his first games after shoulder surgery. In the bottom of the fifth inning, with a scoreless tie, things began to get a little hairy for Gubie, so our bullpen coach, Glenn Ezell, told me to get ready to go in. I was surprised, but I got up and started getting ready. Gubie gave up two runs, but he got out of the inning. We took a 4–2 lead, though, in the top of the sixth. Gubie came back out for the sixth, but after getting two quick outs, he gave up back-to-back singles. I came in and walked Greg Gagne before striking out Dan Gladden. I pitched the seventh and eighth innings as we extended the lead to 11–2. Hal, who'd been on the job for about 48 hours, brought in Mark Davis in the ninth. Then, for some reason, after MD got Gene Larkin to ground out, Hal brought in Dan Schatzeder for the final two outs. After the game George Brett, joking around, came over and congratulated me on my hold. I was confused about the pitching changes, but it's a team game, and we won, so it was fine.

Three nights later in Seattle, I was brought in for the eighth inning as we led the Mariners 6–4. Three up, three down. In the bottom of the ninth, I got Scott Bradley to fly out and then I struck out Harold Reynolds, so two up and two down. I had Edgar Martinez down two strikes before he took a bad swing and punched the ball to right for a base hit. Ken Griffey Jr., against whom I'd had good success, was coming up as the tying run. Hal came out to the mound, put his hands on my waist, and said, "You know you're my guy, right?"

"Yes."

"Well, that guy down there [Mark Davis] is making way too much money to not come in for this situation."

"Hal, you're going to need to get a bulldozer because I'm not leaving this game."

We talked for a few more seconds before I put a smile on my face and handed him the ball. I went to the clubhouse and went nuts. I grabbed a folding chair that was in an area between the dugout and the clubhouse and I threw it as hard as I could. All four legs of the chair stuck in the drywall. Meanwhile, things were going haywire on the field. Mark walked Griffey and then gave up an RBI single to pinch hitter Tracy Jones. By this time I was down to only my sliding shorts and I went back up to the dugout and stood in the doorway, screaming like crazy. Guys hadn't seen that side of me, so they didn't know what to think. I was hoarse and tired from screaming so much. Home-plate umpire Joe Brinkman thought I was yelling at him for balls and strikes, so he called time, pointed at me, and shouted for me to go back inside.

We held on for the 6–5 win, but I'd reached a breaking point. I'd taken a backseat long enough. Hal walked into the clubhouse and told me to go to his office. "I know you weren't happy, but thanks for giving me the ball," he said. "From here on out, you're my closer."

I'm sure, between pitching coach Pat Dobson and Herk, Mac received some type of mandate to get value out of Mark, which they needed to do, but I was pissed. Hal and I had a couple good blowups, but I enjoyed playing for him. Of the five managers I played for, I saw Hal improve the most. I've heard that the last part of a manager's development is learning how to utilize the bullpen. At some point managers, once they're fully rounded, have a better sense and feel of when to take out the starting pitcher and who to use in the bullpen. I don't think Hal tried to do a lot with the pitching staff early. He allowed Dobson to handle those responsibilities. Over time, though, Hal became very good at handling a pitching staff.

One thing I'll always remember about Mac is something he did during spring training in 1992. He gave each player a roster and asked us which 25 players to pick for the 25-man roster. I'd never heard of that before. Maybe Hal experienced that as a player. It's brilliant when you think about it because it shows who each guy thinks would be the 24 best teammates. As we were getting the rosters during a team meeting, he said, "I want to know who you want playing next to you. I expect you to have your own name on there."

During the 1994 season, we'd turned a corner. We were 13 games above .500 and chasing the division. If we didn't win the division, we were sure we would have gotten the newly formed wild-card spot. There was an incredible energy surrounding the team. We played Seattle in Kansas City because the Kingdome's roof tiles were falling off. Since it was a late-added game, the Royals made all of the seats general admission. After they opened the gates, there was a stampede of about 40,000 people. It was incredible! In late August, however, the strike began. It ultimately cancelled the season and, with the exploding salaries as a result of the strike, forced the Royals to go in a different direction with their payroll and the type of players they brought in.

I still have a good sense that Hal didn't want to be part of a rebuilding process. I don't know whether he was fired or if he asked to be let go, but either way he was out as our manager before the 1995 season. A bunch of us, including George Brett, were on an annual golf trip. George had to leave early to come back to Kansas City for the announcement that they were going to let Hal go. Had it not been for the strike in 1994, besides the Royals getting back to the postseason quicker, I think Hal would've managed the Royals for a long time.

The next manager, Bob Boone, had played with a few of us in Kansas City, so it was a comfortable situation when he became the manager in 1995. Boonie was very intelligent and he came from a baseball family. He was an established player on a lot of winning teams. Immediately, we could tell he was going to be different in how he was going to manage. He put a lot more into lineups and individual matchups. A lot of managers today do that, but that was unheard of in the 1990s. Managers today use a lot of technological data, which wasn't readily available back then, but Boonie put together a lot of information that he used as a managerial tool. It was early for that and, to some degree, it hurt him a little. *The Kansas City Star* had a Boone-ometer with all of his lineups. He changed lineups frequently, but he felt he could manipulate the outcome with the lineup and play a chess game on the baseball field with the opposing manager because of what he had on the bench to face the other team's bullpen. He was criticized for it because people didn't understand. People thought he was trying to be bigger than the game. If we'd won, there wouldn't have been issues or anything said.

Unfortunately, we didn't win, and Boonie wasn't given much of a chance. During the All-Star break of 1997, Boonie's third full season as manager, his son, Bret, was in Kansas City, and we were all playing golf. We were 15 holes into the round when Boonie said, "Hey, I want to let you know they fired me last night." I couldn't believe it.

"Now what are you going to do?" I asked him.

Well, he and Greg Luzinski, who was one of our coaches, were living at Lake Lotawana. Boonie had purchased a home and fixed it up. He told me that he and his wife, Sue, and Bull and his wife, Jean, were going to rent an RV and drive around the country watching their sons play baseball. (Tina and I, along with the Macfarlanes, bought Boonie's house at Lake Lotawana.) A few days later, the Boones and the Luzinskis left in their RV to tour the country.

Managers getting fired is part of the business. Everyone who gets hired gets fired. But as players we all hope it's going to be later on and not on our watch. When a manager is fired, you feel collectively that you're responsible for it because the manager never hung a slider or let a ball go through his legs. Normally it comes down to wins and losses. Unfortunately, many managers, like Duke, Hal, and Boonie, didn't get the full opportunity to develop as a manager before being shown the door.

Tony Muser was a mirror opposite of Boonie. Bob was a 100 percent kind of guy. He had very little structure with no rules, but he expected guys to be on time and to give 100 percent. Conversely, Tony, who had been the hitting coach for the Chicago Cubs, had a lot of rules. He was very structured. We had a very different environment when he took over before the second half of the 1997 season. I don't know that it was conducive to running a successful veteran team. Under Tony every player was expected to be the same as the guy next to him. His line was: "no special favors." It didn't matter if you were the 25th man on the roster or if you were George Brett. In reality, that's not the way it works.

We had a "work line" (Tony's words) and we went to work every day at 5:00. Until that time we could chit-chat and have a good time. At 5:00 on the button, though, everyone went from foul territory to fair territory in right field and began our team stretch. It was all business at that point. As a player if that's the way your manager wants to do things, that's how you do it, regardless of your feelings. A lot of that had to do with Tony's experience in the big leagues. He was more like that 25th man than a George Brett. As a result, he felt like it was a better approach if he treated everyone like the 25th man. We accepted it and did it, but it was dynamically different from any manager that anyone on the team had experienced. Like Boonie's various lineups, I don't think the work line had anything to do with our success or failure on the field. It boils down to talent and finding ways to make it happen.

Just before the Royals hired Muser, we were going on a road trip to Milwaukee and then Chicago for interleague against the Cubs. The Royals Lancers, who are volunteer ticket-sellers, got certain perks, which included trips with the team. A bunch of the Lancers had taken their golf clubs on this trip. The players, who were allowed to take clubs, didn't on this trip.

When we got back to Kansas City for the All-Star break, a lot of players didn't pick up their luggage immediately because they wanted to go ahead and take advantage of having a few days off. Likewise, many of the Lancers left their golf clubs at the stadium with the players' luggage. It was all stored in this big room where the club used to hold its press conferences. (When the Royals renovated the stadium a few years ago, they added a media room just outside each team's clubhouse.)

The Royals hired Muser during the break and held the press conference in that room where the luggage and clubs were being held. Muser noticed the golf clubs and thought they belonged to the players. So, in our first team meeting with Tony after the break, he was laying out his rules and said, "The first thing I see when I get here is all of the golf clubs. This isn't a country club; it's a baseball team. So, no golf." Out of respect for the new manager, we gave him the benefit of the doubt and acquiesced to his request.

Players have agreements with various equipment companies, and some of them, such as Mizuno, made baseball gloves and golf clubs and other sporting equipment. Chili Davis had an agreement with Mizuno, and well in advance of Muser being hired, Chili placed an order for a custom set of golf clubs. We got back from our first road trip with Muser managing. We arrived late from Toronto after a rough four-city, 11-game trip to Oakland, Seattle, Minnesota, and Toronto. We had gone 4–7. We had a new manager and had just suffered through a rough road trip during a rough season, so guys weren't really happy. Muser walked into the clubhouse and saw a new set of Mizuno golf clubs, which probably set him off even more.

The next day before the team stretch, Muser was talking to the team and he said, "By the way, I'm not sure who had their golf clubs sent to the clubhouse, but I said I didn't want to see them. If you want your clubs, they're in the dumpster."

Chili stepped forward. "Muse, were those Mizuno golf clubs?"

"Don't know, just had them put in the dumpster."

"If those were Mizuno golf clubs, they better be back in my locker by the end of batting practice or I'm kicking someone's ass."

Needless to say the clubs were back in Chili's locker by the end of BP.

Aside from the work line and treating everyone the same, Tony was the kind of guy that you could gravitate toward. He was a great person, the kind of person you would want to fight alongside in a foxhole. His managerial style, however, was more conducive to the farm system with younger players than it was for a major league roster. Tony ended up managing the Royals until 2002, three years after I retired.

Pitching Coaches

Frank Funk, who was my first pitching coach with the Royals, was largely responsible for Kansas City acquiring me from the Cincinnati Reds, I think. He was managing the Omaha Royals in 1986 while I was in Triple A with the Denver Zephyrs. We played Omaha that season in the American Association playoffs. It's somewhat ironic, but the Royals promoted outfielder Van Snider, who they would eventually trade for me, from Memphis to Omaha after Memphis' season ended. That series against us, Van was a one-man wrecking crew. He tore it up, offensively and defensively. During that series Frank asked if I would play on his winter ball team in Puerto Rico.

After a slow start there, I ended up making the All-Star team. The experience in Puerto Rico was tough on my wife, Tina. I'd leave early every afternoon for the field and not get home until about midnight. She was a first-time mom, who didn't speak Spanish, living in a foreign country. Without me around, there wasn't anyone to help. Even the TV only had Spanish-speaking stations. It was an eye-opening experience, to say the least. So, the day after Christmas, Tina and Ashleigh went home.

Fast forward about 14 months. After a good 1987 season with the Reds, including my first experience in the major leagues, I was traded to the Royals, where Frank was about to be the big league club's pitching coach. The Reds really liked Van and how he played against them in the 1986 American Association playoffs, and I've no doubt that Frank had a lot to do with me coming to Kansas City.

Since I'd played for Frank in Puerto Rico and he was instrumental in me coming to the Royals, I knew he was in my corner. When you're going to bat for someone in a trade, you have more skin in the game and then have more ownership with what's going on once that player is in your organization. Frank and I had a great relationship because of his belief in my abilities and what I could do for the Royals.

When I got to Kansas City, I was just starting to learn about my

I'm throwing here during April of 1995, but during my whole Royals career, I was lucky to work under some great pitching coaches. *(Kansas City Royals)*

pitching mechanics and developing my pitches, but as a coach, Frank helped me a lot with visualization. Players at the major league level are gifted with skill, talent, and ability. Many are able to perform at high levels without tapping into their full potential. Frank was huge in helping me tap deeper into my potential.

The other thing Frank persuaded me to do was to use my change-up more. He had seen me use it as a starter and he coaxed me into using it more as a reliever. That went against the book. Most relief pitchers are taught not to get beat with a third or fourth pitch. With Frank's encouragement I developed into a reliever who could use four pitches at any time in the count.

At some point during the 1990 season, Pat Dobson, who was Mark Davis' pitching coach with the San Diego Padres when Mark won the Cy Young Award, said that if he were the coach in Kansas City he "could fix Mark Davis." He got his wish in 1991, when the Royals hired him to replace Frank just days after the conclusion of the '90 season. Even when he was hired, Dobson got in a little dig when he said, "Hopefully, we'll start accomplishing some things and have these guys start pitching up to their potential." After his comments and how he'd been Mark's coach, Pat had skin in the game. Things didn't get much better for the Royals in '91, as that was the season Duke was fired in May, and Mac took over as manager. I really liked Pat and I think he was a good pitching coach, but in September after the club couldn't guarantee that he'd be on Mac's staff in '92, he quit.

The Royals replaced Pat with Guy Hansen, who'd been coaching at Triple A Omaha. Guy was the best mechanics coach I've ever been around. I played golf with him a lot, and he could fix my golf swing, too, just by watching it. He had an incredible eye for that type of detail. As part of my pitching mechanics, Guy helped me control the running game when I was on the mound. As a pitcher if you can stop a guy from stealing, the opponent then has to sacrifice and give up an out to put the runner in scoring position. The first couple years of my career, guys could steal bases on me pretty easily. I almost didn't make the club in '89 because of that. Before working with Guy, when a team would get a guy on first base against me, it was as if I was giving up a double. In 1989 I gave up eight stolen bases and then a career-high 14 in 1990. In 1997 I gave up one. Those are the extremes, but in the final nine years of my career, I gave up more than five steals only twice.

Guy deserves a large amount of credit for me winning the Rolaids Relief Man Award in 1993, when I finished with 45 saves. He was very mindful of the Rolaids standings and would tell me, "We're going to get you that Rolaids Award." I don't know how influential he was with Mac, if at all, but it came down to the last day of the season. Duane Ward of the Toronto Blue Jays and I both finished with 45 saves, but he had more blown saves. At the time I had a Jeep Cherokee that I was going to sell, and Guy really wanted to buy it. Toward the end of the season, he told me again, "We're going to help get you that award." I finally told him, "If we get that award, the Cherokee will be your reward." I ended up winning the Rolaids Relief Man Award and I gave Guy the Cherokee as a token of my appreciation for his influence. I don't know all of the ins and outs, but after the '93 season, Guy swapped spots with Bruce Kison, who'd been our bullpen coach.

Kison had pitched 15 years in the major leagues with the Pittsburgh Pirates, California Angels, and Boston Red Sox. As a player he was a headhunter and he preached that mentality to us. In the first spring training when I met him, he told all of us, "Here's the batter's box and here's home plate." He then put his wallet on the outside corner of home plate and said, "This is where you make your money. If the hitter leans out there, he's trying to take the wallet out of your pocket. So, if he leans in, hit him in the side of the neck. It's like 12,000 volts of electricity going through his body." He liked to add, "Then, if they charge the mound, wait until they get out close, throw your glove in the air, and pop them. Knee kick them."

The first day I met Bruce in spring training, we were going through pitchers' fielding practice with about 20 pitchers lined up. He was hitting grounders to us, and when it was my turn, I fielded the ball and made a nice, easy throw back to home. Kison reached out and hit it back at me about 100 miles an hour. Then he hit another rocket. I thought he was nuts. He said, "We're going to practice the way we play, and we don't lob the ball when we play." I was pissed off. I took the ball and threw it as hard as I could at his neck and just drilled him. I was going for about 15,000 volts of electricity. He went down in some pain. As he got up, he shouted, "That's what I want to see!" From that point on, we hit it off.

As a former headhunter, Kison stressed to us that if a batter ever showed us up or hurt a teammate, or if the other team's pitcher hit one of our batters, we had to take care of business. It wasn't like Elvis Presley's famous "Taking care of business in a flash" motto of the 1970s because Bruce would tell us to keep a notebook and write everything down so we'd remember the opponent. He'd then add, "I don't care if it's an Old Timers' Game years later. You have to take care of business." Bruce was crazy. He told us that he once hit the first six batters in a game before the umpire tossed him. He certainly hit plenty of guys and started several fights during his career.

Bruce was the best coach for me. I didn't need a mechanics coach. I needed a coach who could help bring out the best. Frank started that with me with the visualization, but Bruce kept it going. He was really good. The Royals eventually let him go because he was allegedly too tough on some of the young pitchers.

I liked all of my pitching coaches and learned something from each of them. Unfortunately, even though I liked him, the one thing I learned from Mark Wiley, who was our pitching coach in 1999, was how not all players are created equal.

Early in camp in '99, my stuff was great—some of the best in my career. Even though I was 37 years old, I didn't see an end to my career in sight. Toward the end of camp, Mark had me scheduled to throw three days in a row and he had me doing a hip drill about 200 times a day. I asked him why I was throwing so much, especially since I'd never thrown that much in a row at all during my career. Mark, who had been with the Cleveland Indians previously, said he used to wear Jose Mesa down to help make him stronger during the season. The only problem is that I wasn't a power arm like Mesa...and I was 37. Mark was right; he wore me down. I never regained my strength and I went on the disabled list because of an overloaded right hip. That ended up being the final season of my career.

CHAPTER 4
ROYALS PITCHERS

Thinking back throughout my time with the Royals, though there were years when the team struggled, we had some outstanding players. That's especially true of the pitchers. The bulk of this chapter is what I consider the best of the best from my time as a player. If I had to boil it down, my starting rotation would be: Bret Saberhagen, Mark Gubicza, David Cone, Kevin Appier, and Tim Belcher with Steve Farr and Tom Gordon in long relief.

Starters

If you talked to 100 players who played with Mark Gubicza, almost 100 guys would have him in the top five teammates of all time. He was a positive guy. One of the guys who could pick you up if you needed picking up. He was a team-oriented guy who'd do whatever he could do. As a starter he was available a lot.

Gubie was a little younger than I, but he had a head start on me in the major leagues. He, Danny Jackson, and Bret Saberhagen came up together through the organization. Even though I was a little older, he was like a big brother. We ate lunch together on the road almost every day except for the games he started. I was probably closer to him than any other player on the field.

He was different on gamedays. He had that game face. You may get a hello out of him, but that's all. He was very intense. Nine out of 10 starting pitchers are like that, but it was a different level for Gubie. George Brett has joked that you never wanted to make an error behind Gubicza because if you did, he'd give you the "Gubie Stare."

He was a guy who absolutely hated to lose. He hated to give up a hit and hated for a guy to make an error behind him. He was all about perfection. You're rarely perfect in this game, but you don't see it from an emotional standpoint. He didn't hide his emotions, which were obvious and visible. He also was a prankster. In one of our team photos, I have a tremendous glob of gum on my cap. Gubicza did that without my knowledge. Once that trick had been played on a player, the one-liner he'd hear most often: "Hey, do you have any gum on you?"

One of the most dominant pitchers I ever played with was Bret Saberhagen. His ability to pitch at that level deep into a game and be as good in the ninth inning as the first inning—sometimes better—was incredible to watch. On the days when Gubie and Sabes pitched, you may not need your spikes in the bullpen because they were thinking about going nine innings.

I wish there was as much information for guys then as they have today in terms of innings and pitch counts. There were numerous games when a manager would leave Sabes or Gubie in a blowout in the eighth or ninth inning because they were so dominant. I wish the data was available then because, looking at it now, there wasn't a need for them to throw that many pitches. But bullpens were much less defined at that time, and the Royals bullpen wasn't what it is today. You may not know what you'd get from your third reliever. Besides, when Sabes and Gubie came up, they were in the rotation with guys like Dennis Leonard and Paul Splittorff, who were established as pitchers who threw 200-plus innings a year. Leo and Splitt were workhorses, and they passed on the "this is my game" approach to the younger pitchers.

Sabes was similar to Gubie with his gameday approach and intensity, but Sabes was more of a prankster. He was more of a kid. In fact, whereas making an error behind Gubicza might evoke the "Gubie Stare," Brett has said that if a player made an error behind Sabes, he sometimes laughed at the guy and gave him a hard time about it instead.

The impressive thing to me about Sabes was his ability to smell the finish line and be better in the seventh, eighth, and ninth innings than he was in the early innings. (That's part of the reason managers left him in.) In Sabes' no-hitter against the Chicago White Sox on August 1991, he knew late in the game that the no-hitter was a possibility and he turned it up a notch.

Mark Gubicza, an often intense pitcher, won 132 games during his 13 years with the Royals. *(Kansas City Royals)*

There's one more thing about Sabes and Gubie. I didn't learn how to throw a better change-up from them or how they approached certain hitters, but I learned more about being a major leaguer from them than I did from anyone else. Immediately, they welcomed me in and made me feel as if I'd arrived.

Along with Sabes and Gubie, another key pitcher on the 1985 World Series-winning team was Charlie Liebrandt. Charlie and I were together for less than two full seasons, but I could tell he was an interesting character. He was our gambling commissioner because he was always putting together the March Madness brackets and those types of things. He also was a guy who destroyed right-handed bats with a fastball that was far from dominating. I came up with Chris Sabo in Cincinnati, and I saw him during an offseason after Charlie had been with the Atlanta Braves. Sabo kept talking about Charlie "freaking" Leibrandt. "He throws junk and breaks all of my bats," Sabo said.

I first met David Cone when we were both playing winter ball in Puerto Rico in 1986 or '87 while I was still with the Cincinnati Reds organization. The Royals traded him to the New York Mets before the 1987 season, so it was a few years after I joined the Royals before we became teammates in Kansas City. Guys like Gubie and Sabes, though, who'd come up in the system with Conie, always had fun stories about him, some of which I can't repeat.

Conie first became a teammate in December 1992 in what will remain one of the great Ewing Kauffman stories. The Winter Meetings in December 1992 were held in Louisville, Kentucky, which is only about an hour from Cincinnati, where my wife and I were still living. The night before, I was going to drive down to Louisville to have lunch with my agent.

During our meal the conversation came up about his signing the contract with the Royals. He and his agent, Steve Fehr, were at the Galt House Hotel, and Mr. K and general manager Herk Robinson invited them to Mr. K's suite to discuss a contract. When Conie and Steve walked in and exchanged hellos, Mr. K walked over and dead-bolted the door and announced, "We're not leaving here until we have a deal."

Sure enough, they had their discussions and agreed on an incredible contract of a three-year deal for $18 million with a lot of it front-loaded. By the time the suite door was unlocked, Mr. Kauffman opened his personal checkbook and wrote a $9 million check as a signing bonus. That was the biggest signing bonus in Major League Baseball history at the time. Sensing a possible strike before the end of the contract, they structured it so David got most of the money before a strike. Some guys, when they write a relatively big check, might joke to the recipient about holding on to it for awhile. On the contrary Mr. K told Conie to get the money in the bank before the end of the year because there were going to be some big changes to the tax law that would negatively affect that $9 million check. Sure enough, he was right. There were big changes to the tax law in '93.

Cone was an awesome teammate. You've read this same comment of other pitchers with the Royals, but he was intense on the days he pitched. On the other days, he was fun to be around. He was really good in '93, but he didn't get run production. He finished the season with an 11–14 record but only a 3.33 ERA. That year he threw a career-high 254 innings, and each outing he usually threw about 125 to 140 pitches. The next year, 1994, he had another terrific season. In spite of the strike, he went 16–5 with a 2.94 ERA and won the Cy Young Award for the only time in his career. He was so dominant that he finished with 132 strikeouts and only 54 walks. Largely because of the strike, Conie started only 23 games in '94 compared to 34 in '93 and 30 in '95 with the Toronto Blue Jays and New York Yankees. If not for the strike, he might've passed the Royals' record of 23 wins in a season set by Sabes in 1989.

Another workhorse pitcher, Kevin Appier, is a very unique individual. We became pretty close after he came up as a September call-up in 1989. Appier was from California, and shortly after he got called up, we were playing at Anaheim. At the time there were two players to a hotel room on the road. If you wanted your own room, you had to pay half the room charge. Ape's wife at the time, Deann, made the trip, so he was getting his own room. We got to the hotel late in the evening at about 10:00. Not realizing how hotel check-ins worked, he thought if he waited until after midnight he wouldn't have to pay that first night. So he waited in the lobby until after midnight before checking in. Needless to say, he was a little stunned to learn that he was still paying for that first night.

Ape had more nicknames than anyone. At one point Mark Gubicza and Mike Boddicker had a jersey made with all of Appier's nicknames on it. Ape's real name is Robert, so we started calling him "Bob" after the movie *What About Bob?* We also called him "Bulldozer Bob." Ape had a ranch in Paola and on that ranch he had a bulldozer. On that ranch he used to throw from a pitcher's mound into the bulldozer's blade. That was basically his catcher.

Ape was very particular about germs and being clean. On days he was pitching, he'd come to the dugout between innings and go through a routine. All of the things he needed were on the ledge of the dugout: towels, rubbing alcohol, and cups. He'd go through his routine of washing his hands, going to the cooler to get Gatorade, drinking every last drop, and then flipping the cup into the trash. He did the same thing every inning. First baseman Wally Joyner decided to mess with Ape one game. So when Ape turned around to drink his Gatorade, Wally stood directly in line with where Ape flipped his cup. Ape started to flip his cup and realized Wally was there. They had a standoff. Wally wanted to have fun with Ape, but Ape wasn't going to break his routine just because Wally was there. Finally, Wally broke. As Ape progressed in his career and became more successful, it was easier for us to figure out his routines and work around them.

For several years Appier was near the top of the league with guys like Jack McDowell, Randy Johnson, Roger Clemens, and a few others. In fact, Ape and Clemens locked up in one of those unforgettable pitchers' duels in Kansas City in 1991. At the time the Boston Red Sox were one of those teams that seemed to have our number. We just had a tough time beating them, whether we were at Fenway Park or at home.

On August 7 those two power pitchers went at it with each going the distance. We jumped ahead 1–0 in the bottom of the first, when George followed Kirk Gibson's triple with a double against Clemens. That was the game's only run until the bottom of the eighth, when we added an insurance run after Brian McRae doubled, and Gibson hit his second triple of the game. As it turned out, that was more than enough for Ape, who struck out nine in the game and allowed only four hits and one walk. (Clemens gave up seven hits, walked three, and struck out seven.)

Ape had such a violent delivery that he was a guy who was hard for me to follow on the mound. When he finished pitching, it looked like a grenade had exploded on the mound. Early in his career, the Royals felt they had to change his delivery so he wouldn't get hurt. They'd tweak it during spring training, but then the season would start, and eventually he'd revert back. Guy Hansen, who was our pitching coach in Kansas City after working through the ranks with the Royals, had scouted Appier. Guy argued that if someone would look at Appier's video and break down his delivery, they'd see that he eventually got to a very good mechanical throwing position. Eventually they gave up on trying to change his mechanics. Guy must've been correct because Ape lasted 16 years in the major leagues and never broke down.

The thing I remember about his pitching style is that he wanted to strike out every batter he faced. And he was good at it. He had a slider that disappeared. Whereas most sliders have a late 45-degree break, Ape's would bottom out, breaking straight down. I think part of the reason for that break stems from his mechanics and delivery. He finished his career with 1,994 strikeouts, including 207 in 211⅓ innings in 1996.

Even though he could be dominant on the mound, for some reason Ape was distracted when a reliever was warming up in the bullpen while he was pitching. If he started to get into trouble or it was in a save situation, his head was on a swivel, checking out the bullpen. I'll never forget the time we were playing at Yankee Stadium, and we had the lead in the seventh inning after Ape had been cruising along. They called to the bullpen to have me start warming up. Instead of warming up normally, I had to put on my turf shoes and go up the tunnel around the clubhouse to warm up, just so Ape wouldn't see me. Ape being distracted when a reliever warmed up, though, brought about one of the biggest blowups during my career.

Appier was pitching a great game at home on August 23, 1993, against the Minnesota Twins. Our bullpen coach that year was Bruce Kison. He asked me in the seventh inning, "If you're going to be in this game, when would you need to get loose?" By that time in my career I'd learned that it was better for me to get loose gradually instead of quickly. If I rushed, I had a dead arm for about a week. Some relievers are the opposite. So, I told Kison that I'd prefer more time. Bruce called Guy Hansen, our pitching coach, and told him that if I was going to pitch that day, it'd be better for me to have more time to get loose. About 30 seconds later, our bullpen phone rang. Kison answered it, and it was manager Hal McRae, calling for me. He screamed, "Don't you ever try to manage a game for me again!" And he hung up.

In the bottom of the seventh, we tied the game at 2–2 against Kevin Tapani. Neither team scored in the next two innings, as Ape went all nine. Hansen called down to the bullpen to get me ready quickly for the 10th inning. After we didn't score in the bottom of the ninth, the Twins got a runner on third before I gave up a sacrifice fly to Kirby Puckett that put Minnesota ahead. We ended up stranding two runners in the bottom of the 10th and lost the game 3–2.

There was a room off the clubhouse where we ate our postgame meal. That night we had pasta with red and white sauce. We could hear Hal storming up the tunnel, and I knew there was going to be a confrontation. He was furious. He grabbed the pasta and started throwing it everywhere, including straight up. The only problem was that he threw it straight up and it landed on him. He came around the corner, and I was the first person he saw. It took all I had to not make a comment because he had these dreadlocks of fettuccine and spaghetti. He told me to go to his office. He immediately started going off about me managing a game for him. "Look, Hal, I wasn't trying to manage the game. I wanted to be helpful," I told him. He wouldn't listen to my explanation of how I was just answering Kison's question about warming up. It became an all-out yelling session on both sides. I'm sure guys outside thought we were in fisticuffs.

Finally, Hal told me never to call him again. I'd reached my boiling point. I grabbed the phone off his desk, ripped it away, and slammed it against the wall, as I said, "Don't worry; I'll never call you again!" Kison came in and stood up for me, but I stormed out with Hal continuing to yell at me. I turned around and shouted, "This clubhouse would be so much better if you weren't such a stubborn SOB!" I went to my locker, drained and hoarse. George was two lockers from me. Smirking, he said, "I think that's the best I've ever seen." A couple of stubborn guys weren't going to back down from each other, but that's the emotional part of the game and losing.

Besides being a great teammate and a Royals Hall of Fame pitcher, Appier, who loves science and technology, is very smart. He talked constantly (and seriously) about building a hovercraft. As intelligent as he is, though, a few of us were able to play a trick on him one night. We were in Oakland fairly early in Ape's career and certainly before the time when news was instant through social media. After a night game against the A's, the Royals told Appier they were sending him down to Omaha— much to his dismay and unknown to his wife. We were staying at the airport Hilton, and there were absolutely no restaurants or bars in the area, so to give Ape a proper send-off, we went down to the hotel bar. Someone decided to do the "shot trick" on him. The shot trick is where, unbeknownst to the victim, we're all doing shots of water, but he's doing shots of tequila. Ape ended up doing 12 shots that night. He was able to make it back to his room, thanks to Steve Farr, but obviously he wasn't in shape to call his wife to let her know he'd been sent down. He didn't make it out of bed the next morning to catch his flight to Omaha. In the meantime the news had hit Kansas City about him being sent down, so his wife started calling to see what was going on. Let's just say it was a long night and an even longer next day for the Ape man.

There's one word I can use to describe Tim Belcher: warrior. He looked at every start as that being his game. He never wanted to come out. Manager Tony Muser took him out of a game at Anaheim. Ticked off, Belch went into the clubhouse and literally turned Muser's desk upside down. I was in the bullpen so I didn't witness this, but word has it that Muser was going to go get something from his desk, and the clubbies had to divert him until they got his office back together. Belch was that stubborn about coming out of games.

Belcher, who spent 1996–98 with the Royals, was old school as far as the way he trained, prepared, and pitched. He had a good fastball, but he pitched like it was even better than it actually was. He just knew how to use it effectively. He was one of the first pitchers I remember being effective in the upper part of the strike zone. A lot of times we'd be talking about how to pitch to certain guys, and he'd say he was going to "ladder them," meaning throw his fastball high to get them to swing. That's unconventional thinking because rarely are pitchers successful when they pitch up in the zone. Belch's fastball was good enough to do that, but his confidence was as if he threw 100 miles per hour.

Belch and I were in the same draft class in 1983, which included another future Royals player, Kurt Stillwell. Stillwell was the second overall pick by Cincinnati, and the Reds picked me in the ninth round. Belcher went No. 1 overall to Minnesota. He has the distinction, though, of being the second top pick in the history of the MLB draft to not sign. The Twins were going through an ownership change, didn't have a lot of money to offer their draft picks, and offered Belch quite a bit less than what was expected for the No. 1 pick. After his agent, Scott Boras, couldn't reach an agreement with Minnesota, Tim decided not to sign. He went to the secondary phase, or the winter draft, which Major League Baseball doesn't have anymore, and the Yankees picked him first overall. He signed with them, but then was picked up by the Oakland A's from New York as a compensation pick. Oakland traded him to Los Angeles in 1987, and he made his major league debut with the Dodgers in September. Belcher had textbook perfect mechanics, which I think made him a more attractive draft pick, and he went on to win a World Series with the Dodgers.

I hung out with Belch a lot. We were at the stage in our careers when things were changing a lot. Younger players, especially in Kansas City, were being groomed in youth movements. We didn't have nearly as much in common with our teammates because we were 15 years older than many of them. It was a different era. A lot had changed in a generation. After the strike in 1994–95, I think more teams went with young players to be fiscally responsible, and there weren't as many veterans on each roster. So instead of sitting around in the clubhouse after a game and learning from guys like Brett and Gubicza, the younger players would leave as soon as they were showered and dressed. As a result Tim and I leaned on each other a lot for companionship, especially on the road.

The Bullpen

With his submarine delivery that fooled countless hitters into thinking they could crush him, Dan Quisenberry was one of baseball's best closers for nearly a decade. He was the missing link for the great

Royals teams of the 1970s that would allow them to reach the World Series in the 1980s. The first time I met Quiz was during spring training in my first season with the Royals in 1988. It was immediately apparent how unique of a character he was. Quiz was a guy whom everybody loved. Whether it was in the bullpen, clubhouse, or at dinner, Quiz was an incredible person to have in a group or conversation.

In the spring of 1988, Quiz and Gene Garber were competing for the closer's job. They both were pretty much spotless the whole spring. When the season started, they were kind of co-closers. In fact, through the first 13 games of the season, Quiz finished five, and Gene finished four. However, they both struggled early in the regular season, which is what prompted the Royals to call me up in late May. My first major league appearance for the Royals was on June 4 with my first save coming in my third outing on June 8. It wasn't long after that the Royals released both Quiz and Gene on July 4.

Quiz left as the all-time saves leader in Royals history with 238. He was the first pitcher in Royals history to record 40 saves in a season and he eclipsed 40 in back-to-back years with 45 in 1983 and 44 in 1984. His team record of 45 saves stood until I tied it a decade later, and then Greg Holland saved 47 games in 2013 and 46 in '14.

Quiz played with the St. Louis Cardinals and San Francisco Giants from the rest of 1988 through 1990. After his career was over, he'd come out to the stadium occasionally and joke that he was the best carpool driver in Kansas City.

Unfortunately, our careers didn't intersect in a way that allowed us to spend a lot of time together in the bullpen, but I think most of his teammates would agree that, even though he was a great teammate, he was even more fun to be around away from the field.

I got to know Quiz quite well because we were members at Shadow Glen Golf Club, so we played golf together on a fairly regular basis. We also had an annual golf trip with current and former Royals after the season. Although I would've enjoyed spending more time with him in the bullpen, it was a joy and my good fortune to get to know him away from the field that way.

When I was getting close to his career saves record toward the end of the 1996 season, Quiz came out, and we had a chance to sit down and talk alone for a while. It was so cool that he offered his support as I was breaking a record he established. It's not surprising, though, because he was that kind of guy.

In early January 1998, the year Quiz was being inducted into the Royals Hall of Fame, I was driving to the ballpark for something, and George Brett called me and said that Quiz had been diagnosed with Grade IV brain cancer. I don't remember why I was going to the stadium, but I'll always remember where I was on Interstate-435 when George called. The news was crushing.

On May 31, with Dan obviously not doing well, he was inducted into the Royals Hall of Fame. For the Hall of Fame ceremonies, the current team would line up behind the person being inducted, basically between first and second base. I was the only former teammate of Quiz's who was still playing for the Royals in 1998, so I led the team to our spot. After Quiz gave his speech, he walked down the line, starting near first base; I was at the other end. As he reached me, he gave me this unbelievable hug. It was very emotional for both of us. Not much was said, but he did tell me that the Royals Hall of Fame doors were open to me next. Much like our conversation in 1996, Quiz saying that means more than I can describe. Four months after his induction, on September 30, 1998, Quiz passed away.

* * *

A decade earlier I had recorded my first save in June of 1988. That was my only save of the season, as Steve "Beast" Farr became the main closer while I was used as the set-up guy. The following year Beast asked me if I knew the reason I'd gotten only one save. He told me that in 1988 he went to manager John Wathan and said, "Duke, I've been setting up for Quiz for a while and I feel I deserve a chance now to be the closer." Duke agreed and gave Farr that opportunity. Beast finished 49 games in 1988 and ended with 20 saves. The next year he started the season as the closer, but he hurt his knee after saving 18 games. Tom Gordon and I had been setting up for Farr, so when he went down, I became the closer, and Wathan moved Gordon to the rotation. (Luis Aquino became more of the set-up reliever.)

Beast was very versatile. Besides being a set-up reliever and closer, he was used a little as a starter after he came back from his knee injury. That was in 1990, when he won a career-high 13 games and had a 1.98 ERA. Beast and I spent a lot of time together on and off the field from my arrival until his departure. He was very good to me and for me. He gave me confidence that my stuff and my abilities were good enough to be successful in the big leagues. He even allowed me to live with him until my family came from Cincinnati.

A bench-clearing brawl started at the old stadium in Baltimore one time, but we couldn't get the bullpen gate open. What did Beast do? He climbed over the fence as quickly as he could and ran out there. He was going to be out there for his teammates.

When he got the nickname "Beast," his girlfriend at the time had the last name of Dootie. So it was "Dootie and the Beast." After the 1990 season, the New York Yankees signed Beast. He became the Yankees' closer for three years and finished with his three highest save totals: 23, 30, and 25.

Part of the reason Farr started some games in 1990 after coming back from his knee surgery was because the Royals had a new closer. Going into the offseason following the 1989 season, which was one of my best years, Wathan called me into his office. He told me how happy he was with the way things went for me as a closer and that he expected big things from me in 1990. It was a great feeling, a feeling as if I'd established myself.

We were still living in Cincinnati, and I remember turning on the TV in early December and seeing the reigning National League Cy Young winner, Mark Davis, putting on a Royals jersey and cap. Davis had saved 44 games for the San Diego Padres in 1989. I was shocked. It reminds me of the line from *Christmas Vacation*, which had just come out about a week before Davis signed, when Clark Griswold says to Cousin Eddie: "If I woke up tomorrow with my head sewn to the carpet, I wouldn't be more surprised than I am right now."

I hadn't heard about Davis signing before that moment, so I didn't know if I was being traded or demoted. Sure enough, I was demoted. I had a phone conversation with Wathan that evening. Duke tried to make me feel better by saying that having Gordon and me in the bullpen was very important for the team, and that it was important for me to not be disappointed. Easier said than done. It was very disappointing. It was important, though, for me to have a good attitude coming into the season. I had to get past that and get ready to be the best set-up guy I could be. It allowed me to eventually become the closer.

In spite of taking what seemed to be my role as the closer, Mark was a veteran guy who was a lot of fun to have around. He was a typical left-handed pitcher, so his nickname of "Goofy" based on the Disney character was fitting for him. It was unfortunate that he struggled the way he did once he came over because his stuff was unbelievable. Watching Mark warm up, you knew the hitters had no chance of even hoping to get a hit against him. For some unknown reason, though, he couldn't consistently translate that electric stuff from warm-ups into the games. We see guys have phenomenal seasons, and the next thing you know, nothing's left in the tank physically, but I don't think that was the case for Mark. His stuff was too good in the bullpen to think that he was worn down physically. At the time he got the biggest contract in Royals history, so maybe he put too many expectations on himself.

"Flash" Gordon and I came up with the Royals in the same year in

1988. Flash made his major league debut on September 8 after spending time at Single A, Double A, and Triple A. (He was the *Baseball America* Minor League Player of the Year that season.) Flash had a very good fastball, but he didn't have the ability to throw it for strikes as consistently as his curve, which made him unique. His curveball, though, was just explosive. It was the best of any teammate I ever had. It's rare that you can hear the snap of the pitcher's fingers or the whirring of the laces on the ball, but you could with Flash's curve. Mike Boddicker had a really good curveball that he could snap, but Flash's looked like a roller coaster, going up and then straight down.

As a player and now as a broadcaster, I like to ask pitchers, "What will you throw on a 3–2 count with the bases loaded?" Most pitchers have more confidence throwing the fastball for a strike. Tim Belcher would probably have said fastball. If I had that situation, 900 out of 1,000 times, I'd throw a slider. Gordon almost assuredly would say his curveball.

Flash showed remarkable confidence in his curveball early in his career. We were playing the Texas Rangers during Gordon's rookie year, and he was behind in the count, three balls and no strikes with two outs, to Buddy Bell. Curveball, strike one. Curveball, strike two. Curveball, strike three. Buddy didn't swing the bat on those six pitches. After the third strike, Buddy simply took off his helmet and set it with the bat on the ground. That was basically a tip of the cap to the rookie Flash Gordon.

During that 1989 season, Flash finished behind Baltimore Orioles pitcher Gregg Olson as the American League's Rookie of the Year. Olson finished with a 5–2 record, 27 saves, a 1.69 ERA, and 90 strikeouts in 64 appearances. Flash was 17–9 with one save, a 3.64 ERA, and 153 strikeouts in 49 games. Incidentally, third in Rookie of the Year voting in 1989 was future Hall of Famer Ken Griffey Jr. of the Seattle Mariners.

Some Royals fans may remember Flash more as a starter, but he was used more as a reliever throughout his career. Numbers-wise, Flash started 144 of the 274 games he played for Kansas City from 1988 to 1995. During the rest of his 21-year career, a span of 616 more games, Flash started in only 59 games—and all 59 were with the Boston Red Sox, his next stop after Kansas City. I loved Gordon in the bullpen because he could come into a tight jam and walk away without any damage. Plus he could give teams length as a reliever. I don't know how many times he'd come in with runners in scoring position with one out, strike out two batters, and then go another three innings. Flash ended up pitching for eight clubs in 21 seasons, but the bulk of his time was with Kansas City. He was a three-time All-Star, including 1998 with Boston, when he led the league with 46 saves.

CHAPTER 5
GREAT TEAMMATES

I had a great 12 years with the Royals. Here's my position-by-position take on some of the best players with whom I had the pleasure of competing. These Royals players made me better on the field and were great fun off of it.

Catcher

During my career with the Royals, the club had approximately 15 catchers. There were a few, though, who were most influential for me as a player.

Bob Boone was very instrumental in me becoming a successful major league pitcher. During spring training in 1989, we were playing the Boston Red Sox in Winter Haven, Florida. It was toward the end of camp, and this particular day, I'd warmed up to pitch the seventh inning. At the time I was on the bubble after having a very mediocre spring training. This was my first opportunity to make the club out of camp, and I was extremely nervous. I was on the bench talking to Boonie, who was catching me. He asked what I was thinking. I told him and he said, "We're going to try something different. Your stuff is pretty good, and your location is pretty good, but you're pitching like it's great. It's not. I'm going to put my mitt in the middle of the plate at the bottom of the strike zone. Just hit my target."

I never thought about up and down; I was always inside and outside. I threw about 10 pitches and got three outs. Manager John "Duke" Wathan and pitching coach Frank Funk told me I'd done a good job and said I was going back out for another inning. This was against the Red Sox A-team of Jim Rice and Dwight Evans. After the eighth inning, Duke asked if I had another inning in me. I went back out and faced four batters.

It became apparent to me that day that if I could keep the ball down, I could make a living. I carried that into the season, which turned out to be my best year and the year I became a bona fide major league pitcher. Boone was extremely instrumental in that happening.

Like most young players, I was open-eared. I talked to him one time about Rickey Henderson and I asked Boonie for the key to stopping Rickey from stealing. He said, "If you hold a ball at least three seconds, his legs turn to jelly, and he won't even try to steal." True to form, I held the ball a little longer when Rickey was on base, and he wouldn't run.

The thing that stood out to me about Boone was his work ethic. He was nearing the end of his career and didn't have to do anything to earn anyone's respect at that time. He was one of the leaders in number of games caught. I can't tell you how many times, though, after a game he'd put on the rubber suit and go out for more work. He led by example. When you're around players like that as a young player and you can see how they go about things, you understand why they became successful.

For a few seasons after Boone, Brent Mayne split time at catcher with Mike Macfarlane. Mayner wasn't a huge catcher at 6'1" and 195 pounds, but he was solid, instinctive, and did a nice job of working with all types of pitchers. When Mac went to the Boston Red Sox for the 1995 season, Mayner became the everyday guy. Mayner, who was a Royals first-round draft pick, didn't have a lot of power at the plate—evident from his total of 20 home runs in nine seasons with the Royals—but he was a quality catch-and-throw backstop. He was a very smart, heasy catcher, part of which probably came from his father being a coach. In fact, Brent started his collegiate career playing for his father, Mike Mayne, at Orange Coast College. After a season there, Mayner, who was definitely a Southern California surfer dude, transferred to Cal State-Fullerton. Mayne spent 15 years in the major leagues. Among his accomplishments, he caught Bret Saberhagen's no-hitter in 1991.

My batterymate, Mike Macfarlane, was not only a capable hitter, but he and I always seemed in sync in the field. *(Kansas City Royals)*

Besides bullpen catcher Bill Sobbe, the person who caught me more often than any other catcher was Mike Macfarlane. Mac learned a lot from Boonie. Both of those guys were old-school hard workers who worked hard for their pitchers. Mac and I evolved as a battery and adjusted on the fly. For the most part, I was better when pitching instinctively. After I threw a pitch, I knew before I got the ball back from the catcher what I was going to throw on the next pitch. It was scary how many times Mac would put down the same number I was thinking.

With my style as a four-pitch closer, I had to be able to throw any of my pitches at any time in the count to any batter. Mac knew that, of course, and there was one memorable time when we weren't on the same page, but I trusted him. I was pitching at Boston's Fenway Park against power hitter Mo Vaughn. It was a full count with the bases loaded, two outs, and we were up by one run. That's a perfect situation for someone like Vaughn. Mac called for a change-up. Of my four pitches, the change-up was the one I had the least command of, but Mac called for it, so I went with it. I threw a 3–2 change-up with the bases loaded to Vaughn. He was so far out in front of the pitch that when he swung he threw his bat over the first-base dugout. The game was over. That would've been the fourth pitch in my mind that I would've thrown at that time, but when Mac put down the sign, I thought, *You know, that's the right pitch.* I threw it and executed it, and it was effective.

That happened another memorable time for me. We were playing the Toronto Blue Jays, and I came in for the eighth inning. As Mac and I were looking at the upcoming hitters before the inning, we noticed that one was John Olerud, who was a tough out for me. During my career Olerud hit .368 against me. He was a very good left-handed hitter who wore me out. Mac asked me how I wanted to face Olerud. "I have no idea," I said.

"Let's try a knuckleball."

"I don't have a knuckleball." Actually, I messed around with one, but I'd never thrown one in a game. After thinking about it for a second, I said, "If we get two strikes, don't even put a sign down, and I'll throw a knuckleball." Sure enough, Olerud hit two rockets foul, so we had him down 0–2. I debuted the knuckleball on the next pitch, and it froze him. Strike three. Olerud was as stunned as I was that I'd thrown a knuckleball. To the best of my memory, that's the only time I threw a knuckleball in a game.

Mac likes to tell me that I got him clobbered more than anyone else. Of course, it didn't help that he wanted to tackle any batter who was headed for me on the mound. We were playing in Cleveland in 1992, when Mark Whiten was playing for the Indians. Whiten grounded the ball to first, and Wally Joyner fielded it. I ran toward first and was ready to receive the ball from Wally and get out of Whiten's way. I was a step or two in front of him, but after I hit the base, Whiten knocked me out to right field. He intentionally threw me. I think everyone was stunned because it was totally avoidable.

I got back to the mound and I was mad. Albert Belle was the next hitter, and I drilled him right in the wallet. I'm not sure what I was thinking because Belle was about twice my size. But he just went to first instead of charging the mound *that time*. The next inning the Indians hit one of our guys. The next game Neal Heaton was pitching for us, and he threw three pitches behind Belle. That ticked off Belle, who was ready to charge Heaton before Mac stepped in and tackled him. Belle was kicking and hitting Mac. It's safe to say Mac got the short end of that stick. He got a couple knots on his head from the altercation to prove it.

The next year during spring training in Baseball City, Belle was at the plate, and I was going to drill him. I threw a pitch that was going to hit him in the neck, but he turned out of the way and hit it, nearly taking out a row of bleachers. He hit a missile. Talk about embarrassing for me. At least Belle was one of the best hitters in the game at the time.

The interesting thing about Belle is that, even though I hated playing against him, he was completely different outside the white lines. We played in All-Star Games together, and I'd see him during spring training and we'd have great, friendly conversations.

Mac spent part of his career with Boston and the Oakland A's, and people sometimes wonder how I did against him since we were so familiar with each other. I faced him only one time in the major leagues. I don't remember the situation, but it was in 1995 when he was with Boston and I got him out. That's much better than the time I faced him in the minor leagues. It was early in 1987 while I was pitching for the Nashville Sounds, the Cincinnati Reds' Triple A affiliate, and Mac was with the Omaha Royals. In 1986 I was a starter during the second half of the season, but this was my first start in '87. I got knocked around in the first inning or two. In the third inning, I didn't get an out. The last batter I faced was Mac. He hit a grand slam. I gave up 10 runs in two innings and didn't get an out in the third. I had a 45.00 ERA. Fortunately, after that game, I got on a roll and was called up in July.

One of the last guys to catch me was Mike Sweeney. We worked really well together. A lot of the reason he was successful with me was because, even though some people didn't think he had the tools to catch, I wasn't a pitcher who had that difficult, nasty pitch that was tough to handle. Sweeney's game-calling fit really well with my style of pitching. I pitched backward a lot, and Sweeney wasn't hesitant to call those pitches with me. So we clicked as far as the battery goes, but I pitched to him for only parts of three seasons from 1996 to 1998. I was surprised when the Royals decided to convert him to first base, which became his main position after I retired.

One of the highest compliments you can get from younger players is the impact you had on them. Sweeney has thanked me countless times for teaching him how to be a big leaguer and then to pass that on to the next generation.

First Base

Wally Joyner, who was on the Royals from 1992 to 1995, is on the list of top first basemen when I was here. For a left-handed first baseman, "Wally World" could go to his right, catch a baseball, and make a perfect throw. I don't think I've seen a more accurate left-hander going across his body like that. He could make that play as well as anybody. He hit for more power when he was with the California Angels, but he still had a pretty swing. He had more than 2,000 hits and 200 home runs in his career. He was more of an average and gap-to-gap hitter here, hitting .293 with 556 hits with the Royals.

Jeff King was an excellent first baseman but one of the quietest teammates ever. Kinger, who played the final three seasons of his 11-year career here, had nice power and he was very smooth with the glove. In fact, though he's best remembered for his offense, he committed only five errors at first in 1997 and five in '98. He probably should've won the Gold Glove both seasons, but Rafael Palmeiro beat him out both years in spite of not having numbers as good as Kinger.

One of Tony Muser's first games as Royals manager, he was standing next to Jeff for the national anthem. After it was over, Muser turned to Jeff and asked, "Kinger, how are you doin'?" Kinger looked him in the eyes and said, "Well, Skip, every time I hear this song, I have a bad game." I think Muser knew then that he was in for a wild ride.

To give you an idea of how unique Kinger was, just look at his stats from his time in Kansas City. He played in 286 games during his first two seasons with the Royals and had more than 250 hits and 200 RBIs. But he played in only 21 games in 1999 and retired abruptly on May 21. The day before, Kinger had gotten enough service time to draw a pension, so he decided to walk away and move out to Montana. Years later, he told a writer with the *Pittsburgh Post-Gazette*: "My heart just wasn't in the game anymore. I always told myself I'd retire if it reached that point." He left the game on his terms to find something else.

After moving to Montana, King eventually bought a cattle ranch. From what I understand, he and his wife and their children live off the land without running water. They're even doing laundry in a wash tub and hanging it out to dry. That's Kinger for you.

Second Base

At the stage of his career when I arrived, Frank White didn't have the same physical tools that helped him become legendary for the Royals. As I've said frequently, Father Time is undefeated. Especially playing on turf, it was tough for Frank range-wise when I played with him. He's without a doubt, though, the best second baseman in Royals history and one of the best in the history of the game.

A couple of the guys who were really good at second were Jose Offerman and Jose "Chico" Lind. Offerman was an all-around good player at second, and Chico, who was a cousin of former Royals short-stop Onix Concepcion, was a great defensive player. In fact, he won a Gold Glove with Pittsburgh in 1992, shortly before the Pirates traded him to Kansas City. He could cover a ton of ground and jump out of the stadium.

Chico, though, was always moody. We had a stereo on a rack system in the clubhouse, and it was generally on before and after batting practice. One day after BP, Chico was trying to sleep next to his locker, but he couldn't because of the music. He asked for someone to turn it down, but no one did anything about it. After a few minutes, he'd had enough. Chico grabbed a bat, walked over to the stereo, and demolished it. That might've been one of his most solid hits in a Royals uniform.

During the 1995 season, Chico walked out on the club. The Royals released him, the California Angels picked him up, and his major league career was finished after the '95 season. Last I heard of him, he was driving naked and intoxicated in Florida at a high rate of speed. Well, they assumed he was drunk. "He actually mentioned that he was a baseball player, but I didn't believe him," Florida state trooper Harley Franks told the Associated Press. "The reason we didn't do a field sobriety test on the side of the road was because he had no pants."

Interestingly, things eventually went south for Offerman, too. The last thing I remember about Offerman, he went after a pitcher in an independent minor league game with a bat. He ended up hitting the catcher, ending the catcher's career. That was in 2007, three years before he punched an umpire in a game. If you could take the on-field Offerman and the on-field Chico and blend them into one player, you'd have Frank White in his prime.

Shortstop

One position where we didn't have a shortage of talent during my career was shortstop with guys like Kurt Stillwell, Greg Gagne, and Jay Bell.

Kurt Stillwell and I both joined the Royals before the 1988 season, but we had been teammates in the Cincinnati Reds organization years earlier. The Reds selected us both in the 1983 draft with Kurt going in the first round. His dad Ron was a major league player with the Washington Senators, and the Reds put Kurt on the fast track to the majors. He was a very solid player and an All-American kid. We played rookie ball together in 1983 and then were at Triple A Denver in '86 and then in '87 with the Reds. He skipped Double A, so he was in Denver during the '85 season and was called up after 10 games in 1986. The problem for Kurt is that Cincinnati picked Barry Larkin in the draft in 1985. Larkin, a future Hall of Famer, reached the majors in 1986 and ended up being the Reds' starting shortstop for the next 18 years. That made Stillwell expendable, so Cincinnati traded him with Ted Power to the Royals in November 1987 in exchange for Danny

Jackson and Angel Salazar. A few months later, I was traded to Kansas City. As it was for me, coming to Kansas City seemed like an excellent career opportunity for Kurt.

During his first year with the Royals, Kurt, whom George Brett nicknamed "Art" after Chiefs great Art Still, quickly became a favorite with his teammates and the fans. That year, 1988, he made what would be his only major league All-Star team. He played in 524 games for the Royals in four seasons, but the Royals went in the proverbial "different direction" after 1991. They had a lot of faith that David Howard would become their shortstop in 1992, but when Howie couldn't stay healthy, they signed free-agent shortstop Greg Gagne, who was a similar player to Stillwell.

From playing against Greg Gagne when he was with Minnesota, I knew he was a good, solid player. When he came over from the Twins and started playing for us, he demonstrated incredible consistency at shortstop. He was outstanding with the glove and could come through with clutch hits. He's the type of player that is hard to appreciate unless you see him play every day. Alcides Escobar is that type of player. When talking with other broadcasters who don't see him often, they don't appreciate him. They don't see his remarkable defense on a nightly basis. Gagne was like that. I didn't appreciate how good he was until he played every day behind me. Chico Lind and Gagne were a really good combo up the middle, which was a huge deal, especially with the artificial turf we had then.

The most valuable all-around shortstop during my time might've been Jay Bell because in addition to playing a good shortstop, he could hit the ball out of the ballpark. Stillwell and Gagne had occasional power, but Bell could change the game with one swing of the bat. The Royals acquired Bell and Jeff King from Pittsburgh in a deal that sent three Jeffs—Granger, Wallace, and Martin—and a Joe—Randa—to the Pirates in December 1996. (Has there ever been a six-player trade where every player's first name started with the same letter?) Besides being a solid defensive short-stop, Bell became one of the best ever offensive shortstops in Kansas City history. He batted .291 with 21 home runs and 92 RBIs. That ended up being his lone season in Kansas City, as he signed with the Arizona Diamondbacks in November 1997.

Third Base

The great George Brett is obviously the best Royals third baseman of all time. But by the time I was in the mix, he had moved to designated hitter. Of my Royals teammates, it'd be a toss-up between four guys: Kevin Seitzer, Gary Gaetti, Dean Palmer, and Joe Randa. In my last year, Randa hit .314 and played outstanding defense. Gaetti almost broke Balboni's home-run record with a career-high 35 in 1995. Seitz played more third base than anybody else behind me from 1988 to 1991. Palmer was solid enough at third base that he was an All-Star during his only full season with us (1998), which was the first of two consecutive seasons he won the Silver Slugger award.

I played with Seitz in winter ball after the 1986 season while I was with the Cincinnati Reds, so we knew each other before 1988. We lived in the same apartment complex and shared a rental car. It was good to already know him when I came to the Royals. We were roommates on the road during my first couple years with the Royals. By that time he was Brett's replacement at third. Seitz came up with the Royals briefly in 1986 and then was up for the whole season in '87. He burst onto the scene by hitting a career-high .323 with 207 hits and 83 RBIs in 161 games. He also tied a club record with six hits in one game. He finished second that season behind Mark McGwire in the American League Rookie of the Year voting.

The Royals released Seitz toward the end of spring training 1992, and he signed with the Milwaukee Brewers. He ended up playing through the 1997 season with the Brewers, Oakland A's, and Cleveland Indians.

When he was with the Brewers, I was pitching against him once, and Mike Macfarlane was catching. I was trying to throw a pitch down and away, but it slipped out of my hand and nearly decapitated Seitz. I don't think Mac even got leather on the ball. The pitch threw Seitz on his back, and he wasn't laughing. It looked like I was trying to take his head off. As a pitcher I can't apologize because I've created doubt in his mind. Bruce Kison, who was a headhunter in his day, was our pitching coach and he was so excited about that. "Take note there, guys," he told the pitchers. "We need to do more of that!" I've never talked to Seitz about it, but maybe he'll read this and see the pitch wasn't intentional.

The other story was while Seitz was with the A's he earned an interesting pitching distinction—yes, pitching—that I certainly never came close to duplicating. In 1993 Oakland was trailing Cleveland by eight runs in the ninth inning. As it's written in *100 Things Royals Fans Should Know & Do Before They Die,* "With two outs Oakland pitcher Kelly Downs got Cleveland's Carlos Martinez to chase a 2–1 fastball. Downs verbally made sure that Martinez knew he missed badly. The benches cleared. Among other players, Downs and Martinez were ejected. At the suggestion of pitching coach Dave Duncan, Oakland manager Tony La Russa sent in Seitzer to face Martinez's replacement, Glenallen Hill, with a 2–2 count. 'I threw one pitch, and he looked at it. He probably couldn't believe how slow it was when it got to home plate,' Seitzer said with a laugh. 'It's in the record book because I got credit for striking out a guy that I never faced, and I threw one pitch. I'm the only person in the history of baseball to do that.'"

The Royals acquired Palmer from the Texas Rangers in a trade for Tom Goodwin on July 25, 1997. Early that season he hit a home run against me, as I was coming back from a shoulder surgery so significant that it made me ponder retirement. It was at home on April 17—my fifth game back—and Texas was up 4–1 when I was brought in for the ninth inning to get some work. Palmer was the first batter I faced, and he hit my first pitch about 34 rows back in the general admission section in left. That made me think that I'd rushed my return. In fact, I didn't pitch again for about two weeks after that outing. It was great to have him as a teammate later that season.

Outfielders

The Royals have a long history of great outfielders, going back to Lou Piniella in 1969 and then guys like Amos Otis, Al Cowens, and Hal McRae. The long list of outfielders, which continued during my time as a player, is largely due to the expansive outfield at Kauffman Stadium, which has the second most real estate in fair territory in baseball behind Coors Field in Colorado. General managers and managers have realized that they need athletic outfielders who can cover a lot of ground.

When I came to the Royals, Willie Wilson was on the short list of players I'd heard of because he'd been one of baseball's best and most exciting outfielders for a decade before I arrived. He was such an outstanding player who could do so many things. His foot speed was amazing. Willie led the league in 1988 with 11 triples—his fifth time with that distinction—and it was such a joy to watch him run out a triple. Willie could do things with his legs that not many players could.

Speaking of speed, the amazing part of Bo Jackson was his ability to make seemingly impossible plays on the baseball field. He was the type of player from whom you didn't know what to expect on a daily basis. You'd purchase a ticket in hopes of seeing something that you'd never seen on a field because of his athleticism. He lived for the moment, the opportunity to be spectacular.

He could run baseballs down, go over a wall, climb a wall, throw you out at home, and do things on the bases that only guys like Wilson and other special athletes could do. It was amazing to see Bo improve the way he did. He wasn't a very good player early on because he had played

An intimidating presence in the batter's box, Bo Jackson also may have been the best athlete I've ever seen. *(Kansas City Royals)*

very little baseball, so he was learning the game at the major league level. That's something that's a testament to the type of athlete he was.

Hunting was Bo's passion, and he used to have his crossbow in the clubhouse. Let me rephrase that: he used to practice shooting his bow in the clubhouse! His range started in the clubhouse and went back through the shower and restroom. He'd have a bale of hay at the other end about 120 feet away. You certainly didn't want to walk in that area with target practice. Thankfully Bo was accurate. George Brett got the crossbow one time and couldn't even pull it back.

On the field, Bo was a walking highlight film. Everyone has their favorite Bo moments, whether it was his first major league home run, a 475-foot shot at Royals Stadium, his first-inning home run in the 1989 All-Star Game when broadcaster Vin Scully says, "Look at that one—Bo Jackson says hello," or the time he ran up the wall at the old stadium in Baltimore after robbing Joe Orsulak of the Baltimore Orioles of an extra-base hit. Two stand out for me.

The first was on June 5, 1989, in Seattle's Kingdome. After Jay Buhner hit a home run off Steve Farr in the bottom of the ninth inning that tied the game at 3–3, we went into extra innings. In the bottom of the 10th, with the Beast still pitching, Mariners speedster Harold Reynolds hit a one-out infield single. Scott Bradley roped a ball to the left-field corner. The ball short hopped the fence, so it was way out there, and Harold was running on the play. At first, I didn't think there was any way Bo would get him. But never underestimate Bo. He Iron Miked the throw without a crow hop, and the laser reached catcher Bob Boone right before Harold got there. We scored two runs in the top of the 13th, and Tom Gordon held the Mariners in the bottom of the inning for the win. (I relieved starter Floyd Bannister in the eighth with a 3–1 lead.) Incidentally, the starting pitcher for Seattle in that game was Brian Holman, who was in line to get the loss after giving up three runs in eight innings. Brian went to high school in Wichita, Kansas, and now makes his home in the Kansas City area.

The other Bo moment that stands out most to me were his four consecutive home runs. The first three were at Yankee Stadium on July 17, 1990. The first interesting thing about that game is that we had Bo, a star in both baseball and the NFL, and the New York Yankees had Deion Sanders, who was a star in both baseball and the NFL. (Another interesting and ironic fact, speaking of Bo and Deion, the Royals drafted Deion in the June 1985 draft out of high school, but he opted to go to Florida State. The Yankees selected Bo in the second round of the 1982 draft out of high school, but he went to Auburn instead.) In his first three at-bats against the Yankees this particular night, Bo hit three home runs and had seven RBIs against Andy Hawkins. His third one came in the fifth inning. In the bottom of the sixth, Deion hit a ball to the gap in right-center field, and Bo, who was playing center field, dove and dislocated his shoulder. Deion came around for a two-run inside-the-park home run after a hard collision with Mike Macfarlane. Wouldn't you know it, when I came in to close the game in the ninth, the first batter I faced was Deion. The collision with Mac pissed me off enough that I had to retaliate, so I drilled Deion on a 1–0 pitch. (I missed him on the first one.) I ended up striking out the side, however, getting Steve Sax, Matt Nokes, and Jim Leyritz.

The dislocated shoulder put Bo on the disabled list, and he didn't play again until August 26 at Royals Stadium. In his first at-bat against starter Randy Johnson, Bo hit a pitch to the fountains in left-center. It was a spectacular home run. That gave him four consecutive home runs, which remains a Royals record.

Another time we were in Minnesota, and during the last round of batting practice, they do a "base-hit round," where if you get a hit, you get another pitch. Bo switched to left-handed for his last round and he hit the ball out of the ballpark. And then he hit another. And then another. He threw the bat down and said, "Hitting left-handed is too easy." That's the equivalent of dropping the mic. Even though Bo's career was cut short because of a hip injury suffered in football, I'm thrilled I got the chance to play with such a gifted athlete.

Danny Tartabull also had a great arm in the outfield and he could be a game-changer at the plate. On July 6, 1991, Bull became the first player to hit three home runs in a game at then-Royals Stadium, as he went deep against the Oakland A's. He wasn't efficient with his outfield abilities, though.

Bull loved his cars, and he was probably the flashiest dresser of anybody. I think he had a different suit on every trip we made. In Bull's first few years in Kansas City, I don't think he was nearly as big as he got later in his career. Bull's dad Jose, who played nine years in the major leagues including the first few years with the Kansas City A's, was not a big man. Somehow, though, Bull got bigger. That's not to take away from his natural ability. He was one of the few right-handed batters in the late '80s who could hit the ball out of Kauffman to the opposite field. Bull and Bo could do it. I can't think of anyone else who could do it regularly.

* * *

It would be difficult for some guys to play for the same team where their father played, especially when their dad was a team Hall of Famer and had been away for only a few years. But Brian McRae, who was a great athlete growing up in the Kansas City area, had the athleticism and mentality to play for the Royals. He was a late-season call-up in 1990 and then really got going in '91, while John Wathan was managing. Hal took over in 1992.

The things I remember most about Brian are his athleticism and his willingness to sacrifice his body. I remember one play in particular in Boston, when B-Mac ran into Fenway Park's center-field wall, which does not move and is not well-padded, and it didn't faze him. He was willing to do whatever it took to make a play. I'm sure a lot of that came from watching his father when Hal was playing for Cincinnati's "Big Red Machine" with Pete Rose, Johnny Bench, Tony Perez, Joe Morgan, and so on. Having a chance to play for Mac and with B-Mac, it was obvious that they were very similar players and very similar people. Having grown up in Ohio, my ultimate professional sports hero was Pete Rose. During spring training of 1986, I got to live out the dream for a lot of boys. For about three seasons, Pete was a player/manager for the Reds and he would occasionally take a couple non-roster guys to the batting cages so he could get some swings. In 1986 I was one of those guys. It wasn't like a standard batting practice; he treated it like a simulated game complete with a catcher. After we both warmed up, he would start scenarios. "Okay, you got me 0–2. I want you to come up and in on me." I'll never forget the first time he said that because I started thinking, *What if I drill him?* Besides not wanting to hit my hero, it might not have been great for career advancement.

Anyhow, B-Mac's fire was best demonstrated in a late July 1993 game against Texas at Kauffman Stadium. It seemed like we had something heated going on every year with the Rangers, and this year was no different. We were playing a five-game series with Texas. We swept them in a doubleheader on Monday. In the third game of the series on Tuesday, Rafael Palmeiro hit a home run off Kevin Appier. That was the strange game because that was the Rangers' only hit of the game, but they beat us 1–0 in spite of our guys getting nine hits against Kenny Rogers.

The next night, the Rangers beat us soundly after Palmeiro hit two more home runs. In the ninth inning, Rick Reed hit Palmeiro with a pitch on the knee. Keep in mind, starter Hipolito Pichardo hit future Royal Dean Palmer with a pitch earlier in the game, shortly after Palmeiro's first homer, and during the doubleheader, both Gary Gaetti and Brett were hit by Texas pitchers. So, theoretically, we're even. They hit two of our best hitters, and we hit two of their best hitters.

IF THESE WALLS COULD TALK: KANSAS CITY ROYALS

After the Wednesday night game, however, when asked about guys getting hit, Texas manager Kevin Kennedy said, "We'll take care of it. We can take care of ourselves." That fired up B-Mac. He told us, "If I get drilled, I'm charging Kennedy." Sure enough, after the other Mac (Mike Macfarlane) was hit by former Royal Charlie Leibrandt in the second inning of a scoreless game, Leibrandt hit B-Mac with a pitch in the fifth. Based on the situation—two on and one out with Texas leading 2–1— Leibrandt probably wasn't hitting B-Mac on purpose, so Brian took his base. (Leibrandt walked the next batter, Kevin McReynolds, tying the game at 2–2.)

The fireworks started in the eighth. We had a 9–4 lead, and there were two outs with nobody on base when reliever Bob Patterson hit B-Mac. This time, true to his word, B-Mac threw down his bat and headed for the hornet's nest. He didn't get to Kennedy, though, as Rogers, Kevin Brown, and Willie Upshaw stopped him in front of the Texas dugout. By that point, the benches were already clearing. "I figured since [Kennedy] was the one doing all the talking that he'd be the best guy to go after," B-Mac said afterward. "Hopefully, it's done and over with. But if they want to continue it, we're not going to back down." If that doesn't sound like Hal, I'm not sure what does. We ended up winning the game 9–4. We finished out that season at Texas and took two of the three games. No batters were hit.

I called Jim Eisenreich "White Lightning" because he had a lot of foot speed. He could go after balls in the outfield that seemingly weren't going to be caught. Eisey started his career with the Minnesota Twins, his favorite team growing up, but he struggled with Tourette's syndrome, which is a neurological disorder marked by tics, involuntary sounds, or movements that a person makes over and over. At first he didn't know what was wrong, even when he reached the major leagues with the Twins just two years after they drafted him. Even though he had a promising start to his career, the tics continued and the ridicule, especially from opposing fans, made matters worse. Minnesota placed Eisey on waivers, and the Royals picked him up for $1 in 1986. I didn't know any of his history before he joined the Royals. Once I learned all of it, though, it made me appreciate Jim as a person.

Eisey was not a household name. He was not a superstar player, but he was a really, really good outfielder, especially in our stadium when we had the artificial turf. When you have guys like B-Mac and Eisey behind you on turf in our stadium, you can make a living on fly balls. A fly ball with our guys out there would be caught. Eisey didn't have a great arm, but he was very efficient in the outfield. He played bigger than his arm because he was so good fundamentally.

Offensively, he hit .293 in 134 games and was selected as our Player of the Year in 1989. Coincidentally, his first home run with us came against Minnesota. He went on to play in the World Series with the Philadelphia Phillies in 1993 and then he won a World Series ring with the Florida Marlins in 1997. "It's amazing to know where I came from— not just playing in big league baseball, but I got to play in the best games of the year and the last games," Eisey said. "That's the highest notch you can go in baseball. The Hall of Fame is an individual honor, but a World Series championship is about the team."

The Royals picked up Tom Goodwin off waivers from the Los Angeles Dodgers before the 1994 season, but he wasn't an everyday player until 1995. The first time I saw him was in spring training against the Dodgers. He hit routine ground balls in the infield three times and was on base all three times. He was a burner, another good fit for our ballpark. Like Eisey, Goody didn't have a great arm, but he could go get them in the outfield. Plus he was an outstanding teammate, and it was easy to pull for him. He cared about his teammates, and the feeling was mutual. He was able to play in four different postseasons with three teams: the Rangers, San Francisco Giants, and the Chicago Cubs. (He went to the World Series with the Giants in 2002.)

In my last year, 1999, the Royals had a tremendous outfield once again with Johnny Damon, Carlos Beltran, and Jermaine Dye.

The interesting thing about Damon is that he was not the most technically sound player, but he found a way to get the job done. As a lead-off guy, his goal is to be standing on first base. He could do that. He hit in the middle of the lineup a lot, especially after leaving Kansas City, and he hit a lot of home runs, but he was a good lead-off guy. Johnny, who could break bats with the best of them, would take the craziest swings and sometimes end up on second or third with his tremendous speed.

The Royals selected Johnny in the first round of the 1992 amateur draft out of high school. After spending the first three seasons in Single A ball, he started at Double A Wichita in 1995 and then made the jump to Kansas City late that season. At the time it wasn't common for a guy to go from Double A straight to the majors. Johnny came up when he was 21 years old. That's a huge jump, but players with his ability can rise to the occasion and do special things. Certain guys, when given the opportunity, will elevate their game and impress people. That's what Johnny did.

Unfortunately, Johnny was given the label as Kansas City's next big thing, the next George Brett. He hit in the .270–.280 range in each of his first three seasons with a lot of doubles and triples. In his last year with the Royals in 2000, he lived up to the expectations, offensively at least, as he hit a career-best .327 with career-highs in hits (214) and doubles (42), along with 10 triples, 16 home runs, and 88 RBIs. After he left Kansas City he turned into a power guy.

Damon was the first in a series of trades that many fans saw as lopsided when he was part of a three-team trade that brought Angel Berroa, A.J. Hinch, and Roberto Hernandez to Kansas City, and Johnny went to the Oakland A's. He eventually won World Series rings with the Boston Red Sox and the New York Yankees.

It was easy to tell at an early stage that Beltran was going to have a special career. You could see how gifted he was and how effortless he made things. He was criticized for making the game look so easy in the outfield, as if he wasn't trying. It was similar to the criticism that the Royals' first five-tool player, Otis, heard throughout the 1970s. Carlos, like Amos, was just smooth in the outfield. He was an efficient runner who would glide to get baseballs. He'd run just fast enough to get to the spot. When he needed to explode, he could. You knew that if he stayed healthy, he'd be fun to watch. In our lone full season together, he hit .293 with 194 hits, 22 home runs, and 108 RBIs. In June 2004 a three-team deal sent Beltran to the Houston Astros while the Royals received Mark Teahen, Mike Wood, and John Buck.

If there ever was a player made for a position, it was Dye for right field. He was a big guy who wasn't fast, but he was athletic and he could track down baseballs. Most importantly, he had a cannon for a right arm. If a team ran on Dye, it was making a mistake. He could rise to the occasion. He could drive in runs and hit big home runs. Bo, Beltran, and Dye were all the type of players who would find ways to do special things when needed.

Jermaine made the All-Star team in 2000 and became the first Royals player to start in an All-Star Game since Tartabull was the American League's starting designated hitter in 1991. Dye was then the last All-Star Game starter from the Royals until Salvador Perez in 2014. It was unfortunate that the economics for the Royals did not allow the team to keep those three players, but we had a glimpse of what a star-studded outfield was like.

Designated Hitter

I couldn't end this chapter without a section on designated hitters. Even though I've mentioned two of these already, the Royals have had a history of good designated hitters going back to the guy who helped set the standard for a DH, Hal McRae.

Chili Davis was a great teammate. He was a good guy to be around for both younger players and veterans. He was a very loose player. He had T-shirts made with different sayings that he'd been told or that he used to say. He probably had at least a dozen different sayings.

I'd played against Chili for a lot of years. We faced each other 28 times, which is the second most of anyone for me. My numbers were decent against him—he got one hit against me—but it wasn't easy. He was a guy who'd go out of his way to say hello and talk to players on other teams. I'd face him one night and then the next afternoon I'd see him as we were leaving the field after batting practice, and he'd say, "Hey, you got me last night, but I'm going to get you tonight." He was joking around, but you knew there was something to it because of how good of a hitter he was. He spent only the 1997 season with us, but he's in my top 10 teammates of all time.

I'll never forget the first time I pitched against Mike Sweeney. It was in 1995 at spring training. We had a lot of rain that spring, which cut back on work for the pitchers. We came down to the time in camp when the club really needed to look at certain players and make decisions on who's being sent where, or if they'll remain with the organization. One morning it rained, and they cancelled the game, so I was at the hotel when Bruce Kison called and asked if I could go to the stadium and pitch in a simulated game once the weather cleared. I needed to get my innings in, and there were three or four hitters from the minor leagues that the Royals wanted to see. In a simulated game, you're pitching like it's a real game, including having a home-plate umpire—in this case it was manager Bob Boone. I had this minor league kid on a 3–2 count and I threw him a really good slider, down and away, off the plate. It's a pitch on which I'd get major league hitters swinging and missing a lot. The next thing I know, the ball whizzed past my head. I thought, *Who's this kid?* Sure enough, it was Mike Sweeney. It was evident to me at that point that he had big league tools, at least offensively. That's when I knew he could be a great hitter. He just kept doing it in the big leagues.

Sweeney was fun to watch. In August 2001, after I already had retired, the intense but normally mild-mannered Sweeney charged the mound against Detroit Tigers pitcher Jeff Weaver and body slammed him. That

George Brett was a great defensive third baseman, but by the time I joined the Royals, he mostly served as our designated hitter. *(Kansas City Royals)*

was completely out of character for Sweeney, but it was a bold statement. That was a way of saying, "I might be one of the nicest guys in the league, but don't put me in a situation where I have to embarrass you."

Sweeney is a devout Christian and open about his beliefs. Manager Tony Muser had the famous quote: "Chewing on cookies and drinking milk and praying is not going to get it done…It's going to take a lot of hard work and it's a mind-set." I'm not sure if that was a direct comment toward Sweeney, but it was taken that way.

Anyhow, Sweeney worked hard in the weight room and on the field. There are some players who are willing to be at the stadium and put in extra work at 2:00 in the afternoon to make themselves into great players. When you work hard to accomplish that, the guys in the clubhouse with you appreciate that. Sweeney had a "C" on his uniform for a reason. Sometimes it's being the guy who'll rally the troops in the clubhouse and sometimes it's being the guy who'll do things on the field. It helps everyone around you to become better. Alex Gordon is that guy for the Royals now.

Gordon's hero is George Brett, who began playing DH more in the 1990s after playing third and first base. Just watching Brett as a teammate, he would be the hitter who would've been one of the toughest outs for me. He was the kind of player who could elevate his game every night to help the Royals win. He could do that more than any other teammate I ever had. He got better with more pressure.

As a teammate we had tremendous respect for George. Everyone around the league respected him. He was an elite player who everyone looked up to. He was a very good leader—not only by his play, but also by the way he prepared and worked. He was fun in the clubhouse and a great guy to grab a beer with after the game, but during a game, his focus and intensity were at a very high level. When you see guys like that going about their business, it's not surprising to see the level of success they have.

CHAPTER 6
A VIEW FROM THE MOUND

The biggest asset for a closer is a short memory. If things are going well, you don't need anything to boost you that day. If things are bad, you sure don't need anything to bring you down. You have to go out day after day and pitch to your strengths because the way you pitch in the eighth and ninth innings is far different from the fifth, sixth, and seventh innings. For whatever reason, the last three outs in a game are usually the toughest. A closer has to assess the situation and get out of it.

As far as my approach, there were times when I was trying to miss the bat on the first pitch because they had a runner on third with fewer than two outs and I had to keep that runner there. Then, I was pitching for a strikeout. If it's a one-run game with a runner on third, the primary goal was to get out of the inning. The secondary goal was to get out of the inning with a tied game. The last thing I could do was give up more than one run. *What's my best way to do that? Who's on deck? Who's on the bench?* You're thinking about that in the bullpen when warming up. You looked at the lineup card with the bullpen coach to see what's coming. Oftentimes there was a pinch-hitter you needed to be ready to face. Being ready to pitch in that situation, you had to prove yourself.

These days, there's so much information available to both pitchers and hitters. We had information on hitters, but for me it was paralysis by analysis. If I'm going to face 13 guys in an outing and I have a pile of notes, I'm not smart enough to figure all of that out. It was better for me to be prepared for the situation instead of the player. I had a good feel for the players because of past experiences. I knew what would be the best approach for me against that player. I had to go by feel and not what the notebook said.

During the second half of 1986 and the first half of '87, while I was in the Cincinnati organization, I was a starting pitcher. That helped me work on using different pitches when I faced a batter for a second time in the lineup. That helped me later when, with the Royals, I might be brought in for a three-inning save and face a batter twice. Let's say a guy got a hit on a fastball in the seventh. I might be more reluctant to throw it in the ninth. But that didn't mean I wouldn't. One night maybe a guy got a hit on my slider. I might go back to it, knowing that I didn't execute it well the night before. So, even though I had four pitches, I could focus on each batter and not try to orchestrate a lineup.

The ultimate goal, of course, is to get 27 outs. You can't run and hide or dig a hole. There's no time clock to expire. You have to get outs for the game to move forward. I'd like to get the outs in as few as pitches as possible. One, it saves your arm. Two, guys behind you like to make plays quicker.

Good things happen more often when you're working quickly and challenging the hitters. Being a closer helped me to elevate my game. There's usually very little room for mistakes, so I was able to get focused quickly and lock into a situation. When you're healthy and rested and on your game, that's easy to do. As a broadcaster now, I oftentimes catch myself making comments on the air about how the game's become a standstill. Many times, it's almost as if the pitcher is afraid to make a pitch. He's not trusting his ability. It can be scary if you feel your stuff isn't very good or you're not as confident in your ability as you were the day before. Unfortunately, it happens. You may know you're physically not at 100 percent. You're still going through stall tactics, not recognizing that you don't have it that particular game. As the pitcher it seems everyone in the ballpark except you is aware of it. I think hitters even sense it, and their confidence goes up because of it.

One time when I didn't have my best stuff and things weren't going well, pitching coach Bruce Kison came out to the mound and said, "I want you to walk behind the mound and have a mental cigarette." In other words, he wanted me to take a moment to catch my breath, forget about what had happened, and regroup.

When I was at my best, I just wanted to execute each pitch to the fullest extent. Sometimes that meant I was missing bats, and sometimes

During my 12 years as a reliever for the Royals, my approach was to work quickly and challenge hitters. *(Kansas City Royals.)*

it was weak contact. There are times, though, when a strikeout is important. Not to mention, as a pitcher, it is fun to challenge a hitter and get him to strike out.

On April 29, 1990, against the Texas Rangers I was able to do something I hadn't thought about doing—and never set out to do—when I struck out three batters on nine pitches, also known as the "Immaculate

Inning." The first and most noteworthy batter in that eighth inning was Pete Incaviglia. One common theme for my career is that free-swinging right-handed power hitters didn't usually concern me. That describes Incaviglia, who had 100 home runs in his first four seasons in the majors, from 1986 to 1989, but 642 strikeouts in that same span. I don't think I threw a strike to Incaviglia, but he swung at all three. I wasn't good at elevating the ball, so they might've been mistakes. Six pitches later I'd struck out Geno Petralli and pinch-hitter Thad Bosley.

After the game someone told me it tied a record with nine pitches to get three outs. Then, a few days later Tim Kurkjian wrote in *Sports Illustrated* that I was the seventh modern-day pitcher in the American League to do it. I had no idea it was that rare. Here's a funny thing about it being rare and me being the seventh A.L. pitcher to do it: the sixth was Danny Jackson during the 1985 World Series, and the eighth was another Royals teammate, Stan Belinda, in 1994.

TOP 10 TOUGHEST HITTERS I FACED

Throughout my career from 1987 with Cincinnati and then 1988–99 with the Royals, I faced 680 batters. Of that 680, 199 of those hitters had only one plate appearance against me. When I look at the list on baseballreference.com, some are so surprising to me. I thought Robin Ventura, for instance, wore me out, but he hit only .211 against me. Then there was someone like Seattle's Edgar Martinez, who was one of the best hitters in the game. He was a tough out, but he hit only .143 against me. I had good success against him because I'd always bear down on him with a bunch of lefties coming up after him.

So, it's difficult to pick the 10 batters I least wanted to face. You may be surprised to learn that the big-swinging, right-handed

IF THESE WALLS COULD TALK: KANSAS CITY ROYALS

hitters usually didn't scare me. I'd rather face Albert Belle than Kenny Lofton. I called guys like Lofton "fleas." Or they could be called gnats. They wouldn't go away. Whenever someone like that was hitting, I knew I was going to have to go to work. Although their numbers against me don't always prove it, here are the 10 batters I would've preferred not facing, along with a few honorable mentions.

1. Harold Baines (6-for-20, .300 batting average, .750 slugging percentage, three home runs, six RBIs, two walks, four strikeouts against me)—He was a lefty who was either hitting in the middle of a lineup or, if we had a left-handed starter, Baines was on the bench, licking his chops, waiting for me to come in the game so he could come in as a pinch-hitter. He personifies the expression "professional hitter." My style didn't match well with his style.

I remember a game at Oakland on August 8, 1992, when Gregg Jefferies hit Dennis Eckersley for a two-out, two-run hit that gave us the lead in the top of the ninth inning. Eckersley had set a major league record by converting 40 consecutive save opportunities before that moment. I came in for the bottom of the ninth inning with a 3–2 lead. I walked Rickey Henderson and Carney Lansford before Baines hit it out of the park for a walk-off win. Not all pitchers agree with this, but my thinking was that if a guy hit the ball out of the ballpark against me, frankly, it wasn't a good pitch. Sure enough, all the reporters were next to my locker asking what happened. (Closers are like NFL kickers. When we do our job in a pressure situation, the reporters rarely want to talk. When we mess up, they want the scoop.) I just told them, "We all make mistakes and we both made one today. [Eckersley] gave up a big hit, but his team picked him up."

The next day I asked Eckersley if he was the first person in their clubhouse that the reporters wanted. Of course, he was. On a funny side note, in 2006 Tony La Russa and I were inducted into the Missouri Sports Hall of Fame. Tony, who was managing Oakland in

1992, has an incredible memory and he reminded me of that game. Thanks for reminding of that, Tony.

2. Don Mattingly (8-for-17, .471 batting average, .765 slugging percentage, two doubles, one home run, five RBIs, one walk, no strikeouts)—In the pre-series meeting, Don Mattingly's name came up. He didn't have any major weaknesses, but his strength was that he was a good breaking ball hitter. We were in a tied game late, and I was facing Mattingly. Mike Macfarlane asked for a fastball away. As a breaking ball pitcher, I shook him off. He put the same sign down again, and I shook him off again. He did it one more time, and I shook him off again. So Mac put down curveball, I threw it, and Mattingly hit it about 450 feet for a walk-off home run. Shortly after the game was over, pitching coach Frank Funk was at Mac's locker, airing him out about Mattingly getting a curveball. Mac just shook his head and took Funk's fury. Finally, I stood up and said, "Frank, if you'd noticed, I shook him off three times before he let me throw the curveball."

3. Cal Ripken Jr. (8-for-20, .400 batting average, .600 slugging percentage, four doubles, one RBI, eight walks, two strikeouts)—For a right-handed hitter, Ripken could handle the pitch out of the strike zone and away. He never hit the ball exceptionally hard against me, but he'd break his bat and bloop it to left. For some reason I couldn't put him away. I walked him eight times, which was more than anybody. He didn't have a hole in his swing that I could find.

4. Ivan Rodriguez (5-for-17, .294 batting average, .353 slugging percentage, one double, four RBIs, one walk, two strikeouts)—Pudge was similar to Cal. He would hit the really good pitches, almost as if he knew what I was throwing. I'd throw an outstanding slider out of the strike zone, and he'd hit it down the right-field line.

5. Lou Whitaker (7-for-14, .500 batting average, .786 slugging percentage, one double, one home run, three RBIs, two walks, no strikeouts)—I reached a point where I didn't go to many of the pre-series pitchers meetings. Here's another time it got me. The first series I played against the Detroit Tigers, we were going over Lou Whitaker, whom I'd never faced. They said I could beat him with a fastball in. Well, I threw him a fastball in, and he hit it in the bullpen. Maybe other guys could beat him in, but I couldn't. From that moment on, I put on my invisible headphones for the pre-series pitchers meetings.

6. Tino Martinez (7-for-17, .412 batting average, .647 slugging percentage, one double, one home run, six RBIs, zero walks, four strikeouts)—Tino was a good left-handed hitter with power. He hit only one home run against me, but he was tied for the third-most RBIs against me. (Two guys not on this list, Juan Gonzalez and B.J. Surhoff, each had seven RBIs against me.)

7. John Olerud (7-for-19, .368 batting average, .684 slugging percentage, three doubles, one home run, one RBI, one walk, three strikeouts)—Olerud was a pure hitter with a beautiful swing. He had outstanding plate coverage. He was more of a gap-to-gap guy, but he had pull power. Sure, he had only one RBI against me, and that came on a home run, but I had to work for outs against him.

8. Kirby Puckett (10-for-26, .385 batting average, .538 slugging percentage, four doubles, five RBIs, one walk, seven strikeouts)—Even though I struck him out a few times, Kirby had the most hits against me of anyone. He hit the ball so hard up the middle that it was scary. It was like pitching in a bowling alley. It seemed like every hit, regardless of the pitch and location, was going to break my shins.

9. Ken Griffey Jr. (4-for-16, .250 batting average, .438 slugging percentage, one double, one triple, three RBIs, one walk, two strikeouts)—The first time I'd heard about him was shortly after the Reds called me up in 1987, and shortly after the MLB Draft. We were playing the Atlanta Braves, and Ken Griffey

Sr., who'd made a name for himself with the Reds years earlier, was playing left field for the Braves. During a pitching change for Atlanta, Griffey came over and talked to the guys in our bullpen. One of our pitchers asked if Junior, who was the overall No. 1 pick in the draft by Seattle, was for real. Senior got a big grin as he shook his head, and said, "Yeah, he's for real." That was my first time ever interacting with Senior, and it was obvious he was a proud father—and rightly so.

Another Griffey memory is from about 1998 when my son, Connor, who was eight years old, went to the ballpark with me. The protective netting at Kauffman Stadium behind home plate went up and then back to the press box, so it covered the people sitting in those seats. During batting practice Connor loved to throw balls on top of the screen and then catch them as they came off. We were playing the Mariners, and their players were in front of their dugout, stretching as we finished BP. Griffey walked over and started talking to Connor and threw balls on the screen for him. As our BP ended, I was walking in from right field, and Griffey made a comment about Connor being a good player. I'm not sure Connor realized who'd been throwing on the screen with him because when I introduced him, Connor's eyes lit up. Connor said to Griffey, "I hope you hit another home run tonight; just don't hit it off my dad."

The next season, we were getting ready to make a trip to Seattle, and I'd decided I was going to retire, but I hadn't made an announcement yet. As a courtesy to Dick Kaegel, who was very good to me during my career, I asked if he'd want to write a story on my retirement. He said, "Absolutely, let's do the interview in Seattle." Dick and I sat down for lunch and did the interview. A day or two later we were still in Seattle, and during a Mariners pitching change, Griffey walked over and said he'd read where I was going to retire. He asked if I'd sign my jersey and send it over to their clubhouse. I said I'd be happy to. Well, when I got to the ballpark the next day, there was a signed Griffey jersey in my locker. It's now framed and hanging in Connor's room.

10. Paul Molitor (7-for-27, .259 batting average, .259 slugging percentage, four RBIs, two walks, five strikeouts)—Molitor had this swing where he hit flat-footed without striding. I threw pitches that I thought were in the catcher's glove, but Molitor's hands were so quick that he'd seemingly take the ball out of the catcher's mitt and hit it the other way. I remember a game against the Twins when Molitor came up in the bottom of the ninth in a tied game with the bases loaded. I threw an 0–2 pitch up and in, and Molitor leaned in and let it hit him for the walk-off win. That's how gritty and intelligent he was as a player. He was going to take a purpose pitch. He knew I was going to come in on him so he leaned in for a game-winning RBI. He didn't even swing the bat on any of those three pitches.

Honorable Mention

Wade Boggs (5-for-17, .294 batting average)—The thing I figured out quickly about Wade Boggs, who was one of the best pure hitters in the game, was that he could foul off really good pitches. I had what I called my "bastard slider," which was effective with most hitters. After the first couple of times I faced Boggs, I realized he was going to keep fouling off the "bastard slider" until he got a pitch he wanted. So I started throwing my "get me over slider" early in the count because he'd go after it and usually ground it to an infielder. (The difference in the two sliders was simply where I tried to locate them.) I wanted to throw pitches to let him get the at-bat over with quickly. I wasn't going to go deep in the count and let him flip 10 "bastard sliders" foul against me.

Joe Carter (2-for-20, .100 batting average)—I did pretty well against one of my old neighbors in Kansas City, Joe Carter, but he did have two home runs and six RBIs against me. Joe would swing at nearly any pitch in nearly any spot to drive in runs. I could expand the strike zone against Joe. He was 0-for-14 against me before hitting two home runs. One of the home runs was toward the end of the 1995 season in a stretch when I'd pitched three nights in a row. Bob Boone was managing and he told me to wear my house shoes to the bullpen because I wasn't going to be pitching. In the eighth inning, Boonie called me in the bullpen and asked if I had my spikes on. When I said I did, he asked if I could come in for one batter: Joe Carter. I got loose and went in on fumes. Joe hit a three-run home run that gave the Toronto Blue Jays a one-run lead. Wally Joyner hit a home run for us in the bottom of the ninth that tied the game, and then Bob Hamelin hit a homer that gave us the win in the bottom of the 10th inning.

Sam Horn (5-for-8, .625 batting average)—This might be a head scratcher to some, but he was a tough out for me. **Rafael Palmeiro** (5-for-24, .208 batting average)—I did well against him, but it was tough finding the hole in his swing. **Ruben Sierra** (5-for-22, .227 batting average)—Likewise, I did well against Ruben Sierra, but I hated facing him.

There are certain things you remember about players you have a chance to compete against and two stand out about the great Derek Jeter. We faced each other eight times in four seasons, and he got only one hit against me, but it was memorable. He hit an inside-the-park home run against me during his rookie season. It was a fly ball to deep right-center field that Johnny Damon did not catch, and the ball caromed almost back to the infield. With Jeter's speed and hustle, he was able to score easily.

The other Jeter memory was from spring training the following year when I faced him in an exhibition game and drilled him in the back. I was trying to develop a sidearm slider, where I would drop my arm angle to near Dan Quisenberry's arm slot to try to create some deception. The pitch was supposed to be low and away, but it sailed into him and drilled him in the back. He dropped his bat and immediately ran to first base. After the game I saw Derek outside the clubhouse, and he smiled and asked, "Are we even now?" He thought I was hitting him for the home run he had hit the year before. Being a pitcher who couldn't reveal the fact that it was an accident I replied, "We are even now," even though it was totally an accident that I had hit him. He laughed and said, "Good. I would hate to see what you would do if I had hit [the home run] out of the park."

If I was starting a team, clearly a winner like Jeter is someone you'd want on the roster. But I'd start with catcher Ivan Rodriguez and middle infielder Roberto Alomar. Alomar had only three hits against me, but he could beat you with his legs, his arm, his glove, or his bat. He found a different way every night to beat the opponent. Then there's Pudge, who'd change a team's offensive approach with his ability to stop runners. Runners couldn't get a lead at first, and they couldn't get a good secondary lead against him. So it was going to take two hits to score a runner from first.

Pudge was the reincarnated version of Johnny Bench. He was a guy who could throw, block pitches, hit for power, and hit in the clutch. Of course, former Reds and Detroit Tigers manager Sparky Anderson, who once said he'd intentionally walk George Brett with the bases loaded, said, "Don't ever embarrass somebody by comparing them to Johnny Bench." That said, I think Salvador Perez is the updated version of Bench and Pudge.

Speaking of Sparky, on July 8, 1990, we were finishing a three-game series in Detroit. We had split the first two games of the series and were trailing 7–4 when I came in with two on and one out in the bottom of the seventh. After striking out Mike Heath for the second out, rookie Travis Fryman came up. He hit a 2–2 pitch about as far as he could in the old Tiger Stadium to center field for a three-run home run. That was his first major league hit. Infielders Kurt Stilwell and Kevin Seitzer told me that as Fryman rounded the bases, he kept shouting to me, "Get that weak s--- out of here!" Excitement from the 21-year-old Fryman, I guess. Kurt and Kevin weren't happy about it, and Sparky, his manager, wasn't happy about it either.

From what I've been told, when Fryman got back to the Detroit dugout, Sparky lit him up. Sparky assured our third-base coach, Adrian Garrett, that he would take care of it. Fryman said after the game, "I don't usually say anything out there. I don't show a lot of emotion. I looked terrible at the plate in both games. So I showed a little emotion. I got carried away." Of course, I was caught up in the moment and made a stupid comment to the reporters, including Dick Kaegel, who was the beat writer for the *The Kansas City Star*, about how I was going to drill Fryman. Specifically, I said, "I know the next time he comes up there I have four chances to hit him in the skull. I hope it's spring training because it won't mean anything."

We were playing the Tigers in spring training the next season, and four or five writers asked before that game what I would do against Fryman if I faced him. I didn't do anything. I especially couldn't hit him after what I said after his home run.

The funny thing is that I never had any issues with Fryman after that. A few years later, in 1993, we were hosting the Tigers in the last series before the All-Star break, and I traveled with Fryman and Cecil Fielder to Baltimore for the All-Star Game. We got along just fine. He was a good guy and a really good player. And, for the record, I never did hit him with a pitch.

Travel

I'm not going to lie or sugarcoat this: although we're gone a lot from our families and there are times you can be jet-lagged in the next city, one of the greatest perks of playing in the major leagues is the travel.

In the minor leagues, we'd go to the airport at 5:00 in the morning to catch a 6:00 commercial flight to the next city. So, for instance, we'd fly from Oklahoma City to Chicago to Louisville. Chicago was a main hub for minor league flights, so a lot of times we'd run into other teams during the layover in Chicago.

In the big leagues, you travel right after a game on a charter flight and fly directly to the next city. That might mean arriving in the wee hours of the morning, but you could sleep in the next day. We rarely had a day game in a new city after a night game. So we could sleep until noon the next day if we wanted. The perks were no lines at the airport because we'd get on one of two or three buses waiting outside the stadium after the game. The bus would go to a secret entrance at the airport, drive on the tarmac, and park next to the plane. Someone would be standing with a clipboard at the bottom of the stairs for the plane, and we'd give our name, they'd check it off a list, and then we'd board the plane. There wasn't any type of security, though there'd be a random search occasionally. Since we took our luggage to the stadium earlier that afternoon, it was already on the plane when we got there. The last things to arrive would be the players and the team equipment bags. That meant that within 20 minutes of arriving at the airport, we were in the air, headed to the next city.

When we landed at our destination, there'd be two or three buses on the tarmac, waiting to take us to the hotel. Once we arrived in the hotel, which was upscale from where we stayed in the minor leagues, there'd be a big table that had envelopes with each player's name written on the outside. That had our room key, so we'd grab it and head up to the room. Generally, the hotel would bring each player's luggage to his room about 30 minutes later. The traveling secretaries had that down to a science. They are so good at what they do. It's like being a closer: when things go well, nothing's said, but they get recognized when something goes wrong.

Before leaving for a road trip in the minor leagues, we would get an envelope with enough cash to cover $11 for each day we'd be gone. A bunch of us would go to the Waffle House between 2:00 and 4:00 PM for the $5 All You Can Eat. That was usually our whole day's worth of food. Nick Swartz, who was our trainer for several years with the Royals, was the Omaha trainer and traveling secretary when I was there. I'd ask Nick for my meal money when we first got to the airport. By that time I think we were up to $13 a day. I would take half of the cash and give it to Tina to use while I was gone. That's how poor we were between rent, food, and baby necessities.

That was a far cry from the major leagues. Before my first trip with the Cincinnati Reds in 1987, the traveling secretary handed me an envelope with about $750 of travel money. I couldn't believe it. That was nearly a month's salary in the minors, and that's what we were getting for road trip meal money. As a computer science major at Marshall, I've always been a gadget guy. In 1987 there was this relatively new device called a Sony Discman, which played compact discs. We were in New York, and I went in one of the small electronic shops that are littered throughout the city. I spent nearly all of my meal money on the Discman and two CDs: U2's *Joshua Tree* and Elton John's *Live in Australia with the Melbourne Symphony Orchestra*. I listened to those two CDs all summer.

Speaking of meal money and the Waffle House, that reminds me of my first flight with the Reds. The flight attendant came by with a serving tray full of salad and shrimp cocktail, passing it out to everyone. I ate mine and thought that was great. Shortly after I was done with that, another flight attendant came by and asked, "What will you have for dinner?" I said, "I already ate. I had the shrimp and salad." She got a big grin as she told me that was just the appetizer. We had lobster tail and filet mignon for dinner. After getting a taste of the majors, whenever I went to the minor leagues after that, I certainly appreciated traveling in the major leagues.

My first flight as a Royal was during spring training, and we were going from Orlando to Tallahassee for an exhibition game against Florida

State as they dedicated Dick Howser Field. We were flying through this terrible electrical storm with lightning everywhere. The plane was dancing through the sky like a knuckleball. Willie Wilson was white as a ghost, hugging the seat in front of him. That was my first—and most memorable—flight with the Royals.

Midway through the 1988 season, we were playing a little above .500 and sitting eight games back in the American League West. We had just finished being swept in a four-game series at Boston and we were headed for three at Milwaukee. Not in the best of moods, we got on the plane for our chartered flight when the captain came on the intercom system and told us that a storm was brewing so everyone needed to sit down and get their seat belts on so we could take off ahead of the storm. Tensions were high already, and Willie made a comment that he's not sitting down. George Brett turned around and basically told Willie in no uncertain terms to sit down. Within about 10 seconds they were in fisticuffs. Steve Farr, who tried to play mediator, was cut on the face by George's watch. By the time cooler heads prevailed, we had missed the window before the storm. We had to get off the plane and wait three hours for the storm to pass before we could leave. The headline in *The Kansas City Star* the next day talked about racial tension with the Royals. It wasn't racial tension; it was two longtime teammates and highly competitive players mad about the way the season was going.

We usually had fun flying, though. I had a set of small Bose speakers that I carried around the American League for at least 10 years. We'd get on the plane and several of us would head to the back immediately. We'd fire up the Discman, plug in the Bose speakers, drink beer, and play cards. That was, until 1997, when Tony Muser was hired as manager. On his first flight with us, we were in the back of the plane playing cards and playing music. He came to the back and said, "Mind if I ask what you guys are doing?"

"We're playing cards."

"Who's playing the music?" Everyone pointed at me. "Mind putting headphones on?"

We thought he was joking at first, but he wasn't joking. That was the end of the music fun on the plane.

Since I've started doing TV, we have had basically the same flight crew and attendants, which is nice. We get to know each other. That makes travel about as easy as it can be for as much as we have to do it. The travel didn't get old as a player and it's not old now as a broadcaster. The only part that's ever gotten old is the packing. Now as a broadcaster, I have to pack a coat and tie for each city, so I might have eight or nine combinations. We're accustomed to the lifestyle. As a baseball family, you know the travel is part of it, and we live with it.

Because of higher salaries, some players bring their families on nearly every trip. The families come on separate flights, but guys today can afford it easier than we could. When I was playing, there'd be at least one trip a season, usually an easy one in the Central time zone, when we were allowed to bring the family on the trip. The number of trips varied from manager to manager. It might be one trip, two trips, or unlimited. Our oldest son, Connor, was at a good age to go and have some fun. He was born in 1990, so he was 10 when I retired. He would come in the clubhouse. The players got to know him and vice versa. Our youngest son, Spencer, was born in 1994, so he was too young to really enjoy it, but I'd bring him in after the games. The boys always wanted to go in the clubhouse and get a handful of candy or gum. On one of the family trips, Spencer was still in diapers. We were traveling late at night, and he was so fussy on the plane. Players were trying to sleep, and Spencer wanted to be up and running around. Then he wanted to take his clothes off and run around. Eventually we stripped him down to his diaper and let him run up and down the aisle. It was so frustrating. I told Tina, "This is the last family trip we're ever taking."

FAVORITE STADIUMS

With the exception of Kauffman Stadium, it's hard for me to pick a favorite stadium, though for some reason I always pitched well in domes. I had the ability to get a good feel for the baseball because I could get a good sweat going. So that includes Seattle, Minnesota, Tampa, and Houston when I played. It's easier to name my least favorite: Oakland. It's known as a good pitcher's park, but I didn't like pitching there. Oakland's always cool and dry, which isn't good for someone like me. It's generally seen as good because there's so much foul territory, which gives pitchers more outs on balls that might usually be in the stands.

There are very few times during my career when I remember the crowd. Once I threw my first pitch, I couldn't hear the fans. The exhilarating thing for me was getting the final out and shaking my teammates' hands. That said, the Kingdome in Seattle was obnoxiously loud. They would play John Belushi's famous "Was it over when the Germans bombed Pearl Harbor?" clip from *Animal House*, and then they'd show a noise meter. The fans would go nuts. I couldn't hear myself think.

Old Comiskey Park in Chicago was normally subdued for White Sox fans, but I remember a time when they gave away white seat cushions. The fans started clapping those things together, and all I could see was white. The white-out with those seat cushions was one of the few times I could remember the crowd.

I had one not-so-memorable time at the Metrodome. Minnesota Twins first baseman Kent Hrbek had six hits against me during his career, including a home run. I came in for Steve Farr in the bottom of the seventh in a game at Minnesota. We had a 4–3 lead with Kirby Puckett and Gary Gaetti on base with two outs. My first assignment was Hrbek. I had it in my mind that he couldn't hit my curveball fair, so I threw him eight consecutive curves. I felt that at some point he was going to miss one. Well, not only did he not miss, he hit the last one as far as he could without putting a hole in the Metrodome roof. We went on to lose the game, and, since Puckett and Gaetti were Farr's runners, the Beast took the loss. I apologized to him. His response was classic. "Don't worry about it," he said. "It's not your loss, it's mine."

I have not made it to Turner Field in Atlanta, any stadium in Miami, or Washington, D.C. Here are the stadiums I either played in, broadcast from, or both:

Kauffman Stadium (played and broadcast)

Angel Stadium of Anaheim (played and broadcast)

Chase Field (broadcast)

Atlanta-Fulton County Stadium (played)

Baltimore's Memorial Stadium (played)

Oriole Park at Camden Yards (played and broadcast)

Fenway Park (played and broadcast)

Wrigley Field (played and broadcast)

Comiskey Park (played)

U.S. Cellular Field/Guaranteed Rate Field (played and broadcast)

Riverfront Stadium (played)

Great American Ball Park (broadcast)

Coors Field (played)

Citi Field (broadcast)

Yankee Stadium I (played)

Yankee Stadium II (broadcast)

Cleveland Stadium (played)

Jacobs Field/Progressive Field (played and broadcast)

Arlington Stadium (played)

Globe Life Park in Arlington (played and broadcast)

Tiger Stadium (played)

Comerica Park (broadcast)

Houston Astrodome (broadcast)

Minute Maid Park (broadcast)

Milwaukee County Stadium (played)

Miller Park (broadcast)

Metrodome (played)

Target Field (broadcast)

Oakland Coliseum (played and broadcast)

Veterans Stadium (played)

Citizens Bank Park (broadcast)

Three Rivers Stadium (played)

PNC Park (broadcast)

Shea Stadium (played)

Busch Stadium I (played and broadcast)

Busch Stadium II (broadcast)

Jack Murphy Stadium/Qualcomm (played)

Candlestick Park (played)

AT&T Park (broadcast)

Kingdome (played)

Safeco Field (played and broadcast)

Tropicana Field (played and broadcast)

Exhibition Stadium (played)

Rogers Centre (played and broadcast)

Dodger Stadium (played)

Fenway Park (played and broadcast)

Bullpens

No two bullpens in baseball are alike. Sure, it may seem like they're all the same, but some have better views, some have private access, and some just aren't that good. Before Kauffman Stadium was remodeled, we had the perfect bullpen in Kansas City, largely because our bullpen was adjacent to groundskeeper George Toma's office. That gave us an area where we could get away from things. After becoming established as a closer, I knew my work wouldn't start for a couple hours into the game—or about 9:00 PM for a night game. That meant I had time to kill. George Toma and I developed a routine where he would come out of his office in the bottom of the first inning—once he was done with whatever he needed to get done—and let me hang out in there. His office had all of the comforts of home—a sofa, a desk, a television, a refrigerator, microwave, and telephone. Plus it was indoors and air conditioned, which was a huge benefit for me during a particular stage of my career when I had babies at home.

People who have children know how difficult sleep can be with young ones. Well, our first son, Connor, was born in April 1990. Our second, Spencer, was born in May 1994, and Katy in August 1997. Sleep was a premium during those three seasons. So, when we were in Kansas City and George gave me the okay after the national anthem and top of the first inning, I'd go in, turn the A/C down to 65, close the door so it was dark, and snooze for an hour. I would start by watching and listening to the game, but it'd lead to a nap. I told our bullpen coach that if I wasn't out by the fifth inning to come and get me. There were certain times when sleep was more important than anything, and George's office definitely gave me that respite. In those days it was common for closers to stay in the clubhouse until the fifth or sixth inning. Lee Smith, for instance, would sleep for the first half of the game and then go to the bullpen.

In Kansas City, there was no way to get to our bullpen without walking on the field, so I made it a habit to get out to the bullpen before the anthem. Many bullpens can be reached with a tunnel under the stadium. If you needed to go to the clubhouse or the training room, you could do so without anyone seeing you.

There are great stories about how the Royals relief pitchers of the 1970s—guys like Marty Pattin, Steve Mingori, and Doug Bird, among others—would grill out in the bullpen. We didn't do that, but we'd find things to do to keep it light and entertaining while we waited. We'd guess the attendance every night and then sometimes we'd come up with certain teams—an All-Tall Team, All-Short Team, and so on.

One favorite pastime in our old bullpen in Kansas City was getting out the hose, especially on a sweltering Sunday afternoon, and spraying fans sitting in general admission. Dan Quisenberry was famous for that. After he moved on, Steve Farr became the hose guy in the bullpen. Eventually I graduated to becoming the hose guy. People today still come up to me and talk about me spraying them down with a hose in the right-field general admission section. After I warmed up, I'd throw the ball up to the fans. I still have fans talk about that, too. Those memories are as good for me as they are for the fans.

I'm often asked about my favorite stadiums in the major leagues. It's different for me than it is for fans and probably other players. I enjoy the history of the stadiums, but ultimately for me it comes down to the bullpens. So, in alphabetical order, here are some of my favorite bullpens and some random memories about others.

VISITING BULLPENS

Baltimore: Oriole Park at Camden Yards was the first of its kind, as many of the cookie-cutter stadiums and the domes were giving way to more retro stadiums. I pitched at the old Memorial Stadium, but that old place didn't have a lot of character. At

Camden Yards fans are literally above you on a railing, looking down on you, and they could really let you have it. They'd let you know that Cal Ripken Jr. was going to take you deep. They were solid fans in terms of knowledge, so they'd let you know that they saw you give up a home run to Kirby Puckett earlier in the week.

Boston: It was always a thrill to warm up in Fenway Park's bullpen. I wasn't a big fan of Fenway Park as a player because the clubhouse was as big as a closet. Otherwise, I loved the environment of the ballpark, especially in the bullpen. The fans in Boston, as much as anywhere on the road, were the best. They were the most conversational, nicest, and most knowledgeable. They knew the name of our girlfriends in the sixth grade. We'd be scratching our heads, trying to figure out how they knew that. The fans there are so close that we could warm up and give a fan a high-five at the same time. Fenway is a park that didn't have a tunnel, so we had to walk across the field. At certain times of the year, April for instance, it could be cold at Fenway and downright frigid in the bullpen.

Chicago (Old Comiskey Park): The visitors' bullpen in old Comiskey was in right field beyond the fence. A lot of the old bullpens used to be down the lines. New stadiums changed that. Comiskey, though, was unique. Usually, a right hander warms up on the right-hand mound, and a lefty warms up on the left-side mound. At Comiskey the bullpen was so narrow that a right-hander, especially someone like Quiz, could scrape his hand on the wall.

Chicago (Wrigley Field): As one might expect, at Wrigley Field their bullpens were down the lines in foul territory. So it's a bullpen where the relievers are basically an extra row of seats with the fans. Although this didn't involve us, I think the best proof of that is the game in 2000 when the Los Angeles Dodgers were at Wrigley, and catcher Chad Kreuter, who was with the Royals the season before, climbed into the stands to go after a fan who'd taken Kreuter's hat and hit Chad in the back of the head. That moment aside, their fans were great. The Cubs weren't a real good team when we played them at Wrigley in 1997 and '99, but their fans were still into it. We have a lot of Royals fans making the trips up to Chicago, especially the few times we've played at Wrigley, which makes it fun to go there. The funny thing about Wrigley is that when I went there with the Cincinnati Reds, I didn't pitch and I went twice as a player with the Royals, but I also don't remember ever pitching there. They've renovated recently, but when I went there as a player, we practically had to get dressed in shifts because the clubhouse was so small. It was also a maze to get to the clubhouse. We had to go into the dugout, up a tunnel, and upstairs to get to the clubhouse itself.

Cleveland: The bullpen in Cleveland wasn't anything spectacular, but after they built Jacobs Field in the early 1990s, that was one of the loudest places to warm up. Remember, they had an amazing streak of 455 consecutive sellouts at Jacobs from June 12, 1995, until April 4, 2001. The way the bullpen was set up, it was loud. Fans were crazy. They were trying to get in your head. After we got warmed up, the noise level was unbelievable when going into the game. That was one of the toughest places to close a game in the early '90s.

Detroit: We called the bullpen at old Tiger Stadium the submarine because we sat in a pillbox-sized underground area down the right-field line. Before going into the bullpen, we'd "ask permission to come aboard." Assuming we didn't get a concussion from banging our heads trying to get in, once we were in there, we could barely see the game. There were only a couple of feet that were above ground, and we were looking through an ancient wire mesh screen with 100 coats of paint. Good luck seeing through all of that and then you're at knee level. It was not an easy place to watch a game. But the benefit is that the Tigers were owned by Domino's Pizza and then Little Caesars, so there were pizzas everywhere. For a couple new baseballs, getting pizzas was easy. The mounds were out beyond foul territory. That's where we'd sit.

Milwaukee: Speaking of food, that reminds me of Milwaukee's County Stadium. The bullpen itself wasn't very good. It was a two-level bullpen in right field. The Brewers' bullpen was just past the outfield wall, and then ours was elevated above that. But the bratwursts were awesome there. For a couple of baseballs, we could get all the bratwursts we wanted. Before the strike baseballs were somewhat of a premium. The bullpen coach had a quota of baseballs he had to keep. So, in certain ballparks we'd snag a couple extra batting practice balls and drop them off in the bullpen to use as barter. We'd be asked a couple dozen times a game for a baseball; everyone loves a baseball. A dad may ask for a couple baseballs for his two sons, so for a trade of brats in Milwaukee, they could be had.

Minnesota: One thing that got me interested in television broadcasting was my fascination that started at the Metrodome in Minneapolis. Whereas most places have a production truck for their TV broadcasts, the Metrodome had a room for the production. After the first pitch, I'd go up to the clubhouse if I needed to stretch. Walking back to the bullpen, I'd stop and watch the production room for a few minutes. Seeing them produce the broadcast was incredible. Over time I got to know the people there. Now that I'm doing TV for the Royals, some of those same people are still working in the truck in Minnesota. Everything that goes into putting on a television broadcast is amazing to me.

New York (Old Yankee Stadium): The thing I remember most about old Yankee Stadium was being in the bullpen for the national anthem. We were literally standing by Monument Park with Babe Ruth and Mickey Mantle and all their Hall of Famers. So much great baseball history is literally right in front of you. I don't remember this in any other stadium, but I'd get chills at Yankee Stadium when the anthem started playing. Regardless of your team affiliation, that was a very special place to be. The only catch is that we had to be careful about a flying object possibly coming from the stands. The objects could be batteries or quarters or beer cans. Dave Winfield had this section that he provided for underprivileged kids, and it was always a rowdy section. I don't know if they were baseball fans or not, but they were teenage kids and they were rowdy.

All-Star Game Memories

Like most young baseball players, I grew up dreaming of playing in the major leagues and since I was from southern Ohio I wanted my dream to come true in a Cincinnati Reds uniform. I was fortunate to have grown up following a team that was full of All-Stars, which included the likes of Pete Rose, Johnny Bench, Joe Morgan, Tony Perez, Davey Concepcion, George Foster, and Ken Griffey Sr., to name a few. During my time with the Royals, I earned three American League All-Star team berths.

My first All-Star Game was in Jack Murphy Stadium in 1992. During the American League's 13–6 victory, I remember that Ken Griffey Jr. was the Most Valuable Player of the game. I pitched two-thirds of an inning in the game and left with two runners on base. They scored when Rick Aguilera relieved me and gave up an opposite field home run to Will Clark, who was the first batter Aguilera faced after replacing me in the game.

After traveling with manager Hal McRae, who was named as a coach in the game, from Milwaukee to San Diego with a stop in Las Vegas, we arrived at the Marriott Marquis and Marina, which was the spectacular team hotel. One of the things I remember was the amount of activities going on in connection with the All-Star Game itself. There seemed to be activities and parties taking place around the clock. As a first-time All-Star, I felt almost obligated to attend every event that I was invited to. That meant that by the end of the All-Star break, I needed a break. Before my teammates attended their first All-Star Game, one bit of advice I always passed on in later years was to enjoy as many events and activities as they could but not to get worn out trying to do everything.

The Home Run Derby on Monday evening before the All-Star Game was the highlight of the trip for me. Being on the field to cheer Mark McGwire, Joe Carter, Cal Ripken Jr., and Ken Griffey Jr. was a blast. Seeing McGwire hit 12 home runs during the contest was unreal. He hit line drives that reached the stands in what seemed like less than a second, as well as long, towering shots that could have made it rain.

I was selected the next year as well when the All-Star Game was held in Oriole Park at Camden Yards in Baltimore, Maryland. I enjoyed the 1993 All-Star Game more than any of the three I was selected to for a number of reasons. One big reason was that the ballpark was my second favorite behind Kauffman Stadium, and because of that venue, I knew it would be a great experience. The ballpark had opened the season before and had been given great reviews by everyone who had seen it. Another reason I enjoyed this All-Star Game so much was because I knew more about what to expect since it was my second selection. I was able to enjoy time with my family more than the previous year, and everything was within walking distance from the team hotel. Several activities, including the All-Star Gala, took place at Baltimore's Inner Harbor.

My locker was in a corner next to Kirby Puckett and Ripken Jr., which was especially cool because Kirby was a non-stop trash talker to everyone. (Interestingly enough, Puckett and Ripken went into the Baseball Hall of Fame the same year, which happened to be the same year that Denny Matthews won the Ford C. Frick Award.) Puckett never let anyone off easy, including vice president Al Gore. I remember Puckett giving the vice president a hard time about the new higher tax rate the Clinton administration had just implemented, which obviously impacted most every player in the room. Gore was speechless when Kirby posed the question as to why they made the higher tax retroactive by one year.

At the All-Star Game, you're asked to sign a lot of memorabilia—posters, bats, balls, etc.—for sponsors. All of these items were in a room set up for us to sign. Additionally, players receive three dozen baseballs with the All-Star Game insignia. They'd take the balls back to their cities to have the All-Stars sign them when each went through town. Since we were signing so many things for sponsors, it allowed us to just sign a few dozen balls during a series later in the season. Junior left his three dozen balls on the table with the sponsor items. Guys gave him grief about it, but they signed his baseballs. Later that season the Seattle Mariners, which had Junior and Randy Johnson on the All-Star squad, came to Kansas City. I sent my three boxes of balls to their clubhouse and asked the clubhouse attendant, Chuck Hawke, if he'd make sure they got signed. The last day of the series, I asked Chuck if the balls were signed. He said Johnson did but Griffey didn't. "The Kid said he's not signing anything else," Chuck reported to me. I told him I'd get the balls after the series.

In the first inning of the game, Junior hit a home run into our bullpen off Tom Gordon. The ground crew was in our bullpen, and as the ball went up the tunnel, guys were scrambling for it. One guy came back with the ball and gave it to me. Still ticked about Griffey not signing the All-Star balls, I flipped it into the fountains. As the ball was about to splash, we heard over the public address system: "The Kansas City Royals would like to congratulate Ken Griffey Jr. on breaking the Seattle Mariners single-season home run record." Yep, that was Junior's 33rd homer of the season, breaking Gorman Thomas' record. (Griffey went on to hit another 12 home runs that season.) A few minutes later, someone from our press box called the bullpen to get the ball. Instead of fishing the ball out of the fountain, I went to our ball bag, grabbed a brand new pearl, rubbed it up, and sent it up as the home-run ball. As far as I know, Griffey never found out. And the actual home-run ball? One of the ground crew members,

Playing in my second All-Star Game, which was in 1993 at Oriole Park, represented a special experience for me. I am in the second row. *(Jeff Montgomery)*

Johnny Reed, went swimming for it and last I heard he still has it. By the way, when I got the boxes of All-Star balls back, Griffey had signed them.

Lining up on the foul line for introductions—with Griffey and others—with the baseball world watching on television was very memorable in each All-Star Game, but what followed in Baltimore was most special, as Geddy Lee of Rush sang the Canadian national anthem, and James Earl Jones followed by reciting the United States national anthem in his big, deep voice.

The game itself went well for our American League squad as we won the game 9–3. I was fortunate to pitch a scoreless inning, including a strikeout of Darren Daulton. I remember I was able to use all four of my pitches (fastball, curveball, change-up, and slider) to record the strikeout.

My final All-Star Game was in 1996 at Philadelphia's Veterans Stadium. After posting good numbers in the first half of the 1996 season I was selected by Mike Hargrove of the Cleveland Indians to be in his bullpen as the Royals representative for the game. Our manager, Bob Boone, and trainer Nick Swartz were also selected to represent the American League.

The Home Run Derby was the most memorable element of the '96 All-Star celebration as Barry Bonds outdueled McGwire. It was the first year the derby had multiple rounds, which added a new twist to the event. The Home Run Derby was not the only contest the National League won that year. They also won the All-Star Game by a score of 6–0. Philadelphia native Mike Piazza, who was the Los Angeles Dodgers' 62nd round draft choice, had quite a homecoming and won the All-Star Game MVP after hitting a towering home run that helped the National League prevail.

In retrospect, having these chances to represent the Kansas City Royals in the Midsummer Classics were some of my biggest thrills in my career. The chance to play baseball with and against the great players in the game was a truly unforgettable experience. The opportunity to share a clubhouse and mingle with the players you try so hard to beat each night during the season is even more special, even if it lasts for just a few days in the middle of the summer.

CHAPTER 7:

GREAT GAMES
AND MEMORABLE
MOMENTS

I've never been able to figure out why it is, but the last three outs in a game are generally the toughest. One time we were playing at Jacobs Field in Cleveland, which was a tough place to close a game. It would come alive with a playoff environment at the end of games. Making matters worse, the Indians had a lineup that wouldn't stop. There were no easy outs. This particular series, I was on the shelf for a day or two after pitching three days in a row. We had a left-handed reliever named Billy Brewer who was throwing the ball really well. Billy and Rusty Meacham had been working together, left-hander and right-hander, as my set-up guys. They were doing a remarkable job.

I was sitting in the bullpen with them, talking them through the Cleveland lineup. Billy was called on to close out the game. Things got hairy, but he got Albert Belle for the final out on a ball that Belle hit as far as he could without it leaving the ballpark. We were in the clubhouse afterward, high-fiving each other. Billy, who got the save, said, "Man, you can have that job back. I don't want any part of that; it's too much."

Some of my saves were more memorable than others. The numbers that represent milestone saves during my career are one, 45, 100, 200, 239, 300, 304. The funny thing, though, is that not all of them were particularly memorable. I can say that I gave the final gameball from each of those saves to my dad. To go full circle, when I retired my dad and mom had a big crystal bowl with a plate on top that had holes for each ball to sit in. And then they had a metal label engraved with information from each game. That's a very special gift that I keep in my office.

My first career save came with the Royals on June 8, 1988, against the Oakland A's. With a 5–4 lead, I came in for Bret Saberhagen with one out in the eighth and Gene Nelson, pinch-running for Don Baylor, on first base. Dave Henderson grounded a ball to Frank White, who started a 4–6–3 double play, getting us out of that inning. I came back out for the ninth and retired the A's in order. That was the first save of my career and the only one I'd get in 1988, thanks to Steve Farr, who lobbied with manager John Wathan for a chance to close.

In 1993 I tied Dan Quisenberry's Royals record of 45 saves in a season. And I did it on the last day of the season. I was in a chase with Duane Ward of the Toronto Blue Jays for the American League Rolaids Relief Man Award. I wanted to get the award, but pitching coach Guy Hansen *really* wanted me to get it. I didn't have to pitch on the last day of the season in Texas because Ward had 45 saves already, but he had blown more. With me sitting at 44, Guy asked me before the game if I wanted to pitch. "Don't sit me because I could lose the Rolaids Award, but don't pitch me to get a 45th save. Just pitch me however you normally would," I said.

In the bottom of the ninth with a 4–1 lead, they brought me in for Kevin Appier. I had a 1–2–3 inning, getting Doug Strange to fly out, Rafael Palmeiro to strike out, and Juan Gonzalez to ground out to shortstop Greg Gagne. Five pitches, and we're all shaking hands. I asked our first baseman, Bob Hamelin, for the ball, but he said, "I gave it to [umpire] Dale Scott." I tracked down Dale and asked him for the ball. "I wanted it because it's the last out recorded in Arlington Stadium," he told me. When I explained the situation and how I was giving milestone save balls to my dad, Dale agreed to give it to me.

The win gave me a career-high 45 saves, which tied Quiz's single-season record, but it also sealed the Rolaids Relief Man Award. The main reason I was excited about that is because I got a $50,000 check from Rolaids that I was able to donate to Give Kids the World, an organization near Disney World that has a 79-acre resort for kids with life-threatening illnesses. The charity gives them a chance to visit the theme parks in central Florida for free. Looking back on it, I'm floored and humbled that I could make a small donation to help so many children enjoy Disney. It's a very cool program.

It didn't come easily, but I got my 300th career save on August 25, 1999, at Kauffman Stadium against the Baltimore Orioles. Belle hit a ground ball to Rey Sanchez, who threw it to first baseman Mike Sweeney for the last out. I think Sweeney was more excited than I was. I didn't do anything different on save No. 300 than I did on the other 299, but Sweeney was very animated, very excited. That was his style. He was an enthusiastic player.

After the game, the Royals held a press conference. I'd been struggling the whole year and actually failed to get my 300th the night before, blowing a save in a game that we'd go on to lose. During the press conference, I said it wasn't the cleanest save, but "I guess it was very typical of my career." I added that it reminded me of George Brett's 3,000th hit because, like George's 3000th hit, my save wasn't clean. Afterward I was in the clubhouse and *The Kansas City Star* columnist Jason Whitlock, with whom I had a professional relationship largely through WHB radio, walked over to me and said, "Don't read the paper tomorrow."

"Why not?"

"Because I'm going to bury you."

The next morning I walked into the kitchen, where my family was gathered. My dad was at the breakfast table, reading the paper. I could tell he was frustrated about something. When I told everyone good morning, Dad immediately said something like, "If that guy was working for me, he'd be off the air today and wouldn't be doing anything of significance again at the station." I knew immediately he was talking about Whitlock.

Although I never read it, in the column Whitlock apparently interpreted my making that comment about George to me equating a 300th save to a 3,000th hit. In no stretch of the imagination is that what I was trying to do. Even though I was only the 10th person in major league history to save 300 games and the first to get all of them with one club, 3,000 hits is a bigger accomplishment. I've always felt that way. My comment about George's 3,000th was simply talking about how it wasn't the prettiest hit he'd ever gotten. The 300th save definitely wasn't the prettiest one I'd ever gotten.

Jason was paid to write columns, to give his opinion, so he was doing his job. Everybody has a job to do. However you do it is fine with me. But I don't have to read it or listen to it.

Instead of the negativity of Whitlock's column, here are the memories I'm going to carry from that save: manager Tony Muser got tossed during the game, so his bench coach, Jamie Quirk, was acting manager and brought me in for the save. Guess who caught my first save in 1988? Yes, Jamie. I'm going to remember a big group of my friends who had been in the first-base dugout suite that night. I walked off the field and gave them a ball from the game, and they signed it for me. I still have that baseball signed in my trophy case. And then Sweeney's reaction was, of course, priceless. Those are the memories I carry the most from that night.

Grand Slams

During my major league career, I gave up 81 home runs but only two grand slams. Of course, each one was memorable in its own way.

We were playing the Baltimore Orioles in a doubleheader at Royals Stadium on June 23, 1991. In the first game, I replaced Steve Crawford in the top of the eighth inning. Shag had just come in for Mike Magnante with us leading 5–1. By the time Hal McRae handed me the ball, Shag had given up two doubles and a triple to the first three batters in the inning. Baltimore trailed 5–3 with Sam Horn on second base. I gave up one more run that inning, and we were leading 8–4 when I came back out for the ninth. In the ninth inning, I walked Kansas City native David Segui and struck out Mike Devereaux but then loaded the bases after giving up back-to-back singles to Brady Anderson and Cal Ripken Jr. That brought up Chris Hoiles. After I threw the first two pitches for balls, pitching coach Frank Funk came out to the mound. He said, "Look, see that guy over there, he's got no chance. Let's go after [Hoiles]. If you throw him a fastball down the middle, he's not going to hit it. He'll dribble it for a double play. He's not going to hit a home run. If he does, I'll kiss your ass." On the next pitch, Hoiles launched a grand slam. As Hoiles was rounding the bases, I bent over toward Frank and kept pointing to my butt.

The next one I gave up happened to be the last home run anyone hit against me. It was toward the end of the 1999 season, on September 27, to be exact, and I knew I was done in about a week. Detroit led 4–2 in the seventh when the bullpen phone rang. It was Tony Muser: "Get Monty ready. He has the eighth." In this situation it was weird for me to go in, but it was the last game at the old Tiger Stadium, so my guess was that Tony wanted to let me pitch there one more time. When it was full, which it was that afternoon with more than 43,000 people, the stadium could be electric because the seats were so close to the field. It definitely was during that last game. Flashbulbs went off throughout the game—remember, this was before everyone had a cell phone that doubled as a camera.

I replaced Alvin Morman in the bottom of the eighth and gave up a double to Dean Palmer and a single to Damion Easley before intentionally walking Karim Garcia to load the bases. After getting Gabe Kapler to ground into a fielder's choice, Robert Fick, whom I'd never heard of, came up. Fick hit the first pitch to right—out of Tiger Stadium. The camera flashbulbs went nuts. It looked like a massive 1970s disco party. The stadium almost tore itself down it was so crazy in there.

The 1991 Season

Kirk Gibson was on our team in 1991. Gibby was—we'll just say—an intense player. Anyone who played with Gibby had to learn a lot from him because of the way he went about his business. He was a caged animal and he expected his teammates to play the same way. If there was a fight, Gibby was a guy that I would want on my side because the only way we'd lose is if they literally killed him.

We had a beanball game going with Texas, which isn't a shock because we always seemed to have skirmishes with the Rangers. This particular night at the old ballpark in Arlington, George Brett was at the plate and he got knocked to the ground on two or three consecutive pitches. It happened again in another at-bat. That meant one of the Rangers was going down. After Kevin Appier started the game, Luis Aquino was pitching the final four innings. There were numerous times when he could've drilled someone, but he didn't. After the game, which we won 12–5, the clubhouse attitude was down. We were happy that we'd won, but there was an empty feeling because our Hall of Fame player was dusting himself off a lot that night without any recourse.

Next thing you know, Gibby came storming in the clubhouse, bat in hand. It was obvious he'd taken out his frustration already with this bat. He was sweating, and his face was bright red with the veins in his neck popping out. He got on the picnic table that had our postgame food spread and swung the bat around, screaming: "I don't know what I'm doing on this f-----g team! You're a bunch of f-----g p-----s!" Then he pointed the bat at George. "For your information, that is George f-----g Brett! No. 5! Future Hall of Famer! He got knocked on his ass, and not one pitcher did anything to stop that!" Aquino, whose locker was next to mine, leaned over and said quietly to me, "I couldn't retaliate. I had to protect my ERA."

"Shh, Luis, don't say anything; Gibby will kill you!"

Gibby was that intense. He left his mark in our clubhouse bathroom on Opening Day of '91. He was fired up and ready to play. He went into the bathroom with his bat and started beating on the wall tile in the bathroom. For a couple years, there was a Sharpie circle around the hole that read: "Gibby was here."

That year also featured Bret Saberhagen's no-hitter on August 26, 1991. The scary thought was that he was probably better in the seventh, eighth, and ninth innings than he was in the first six. That was true of most of his starts. If guys like Sabes, Roger Clemens, Randy Johnson, and Pedro Martinez got the ball late in the game, especially with a lead, you can turn the lights out. They'll sniff out the finish line. When Sabes pitched, I'd know by the middle of the game if I'd be in there that night. If he was matched up with another high-profile pitcher, it'd be a close game, and there's a good chance I'd be in there. But if he got five runs, it's over. The no-hitter was a 7–0 blowout against the Chicago White Sox. We got five runs in the first three innings, so it was basically over after that. The final out was a ground ball from Frank Thomas to second baseman Terry Shumpert.

Usually when a pitcher throws a no-hitter, he points to at least one or two plays from the game that saved the no-hitter. There was one in particular that might've saved Sabes. In the top of the fifth inning, Dan Pasqua hit a fly ball to left field. Originally it was ruled a double, but later in the game, it was changed to an error on left fielder Kirk Gibson. Gibby was pissed that he got an error.

From the bullpen angle, the impressive thing was the way Sabes used his fastball late in that game. He could pinpoint his fastball inside better than anyone I've seen and he was doing it in that game. Sabes was probably hitting the high 90s late in the game. After a quick celebration in the middle of the field, we went to the clubhouse and enjoyed a nice champagne celebration for Sabes in there.

Saberhagen was an excellent pitcher, and I had an amusing encounter with another pitching great. During the second half of the 1986 season, I was playing for the Denver Zephyrs, the Triple A affiliate at the time for the Cincinnati Reds. We were on a road trip playing against the Iowa Cubs in Des Moines. That season I was a starting pitcher and had pitched the night before, which meant I was on the "bucket" during batting practice before our next game. The primary responsibility for the pitcher manning the bucket is to collect all of the baseballs that are hit during batting practice, which are rolled by the guys shagging balls in the outfield, into the area in shallow center field.

The "bucket" was such a terrible responsibility that starting pitchers, who like me were struggling to pay rent, would offer $5 to a batboy to help him on the bucket. On this particular day, I asked one of the batboys for the Iowa Cubs to help me on the bucket. When I asked, he gave me a vacant stare. I then told him I would tip him $5 if he would help me. That drew another blank stare and a head shake as if I was a moron.

After batting practice and a quick change into our game uniforms, we were ready for the national anthem. Standing on the top step of the dugout, I noticed the "batboy" I had asked to man the bucket for me was out around the pitcher's mound area. It seemed odd timing for him to be out there, but I assumed he was delivering the rosin bag for the pitchers to use that night.

Very quickly I learned that the kid I assumed was a batboy was far from such. That "kid" proceeded to toss nine innings of shutout baseball against our Denver team. His name was Greg Maddux. He was 20 years old at the time and making his first Triple A start after being called up from Double A. He went on to have a 10–1 record at Triple A that year and earned a September call-up to Chicago, where he made his major league debut.

Comebacks

The Royals of recent years, particularly the 2014 and '15 clubs, have displayed a never-say-die attitude. The size of the deficit doesn't seem to matter. Ninth inning with one out? No big deal. They can do it. But one of the biggest comeback wins in club history happened during my last season.

We were getting smoked at home by the Cleveland Indians 7–1 on June 26, 1999. Every day I'd go to the ballpark and get my workout in around 4:00, but if I couldn't, I'd do it afterward. I didn't do it that day, so after my 13-pitch inning of work, I figured I was done since it was such a lopsided contest. I took off my uniform, put on my workout clothes, and hopped on the treadmill for a four-mile run. There was a TV in the weight room, so I started watching the game. Suddenly, in the bottom of the eighth, a couple guys reached with one out, and the bases were loaded. And then one run scored on a base hit by Carlos Beltran. Later in the inning, Jermaine Dye hit a two-run double. Chad Kreuter hit a bases-clearing double that scored three. In the blink of an eye, we scored 10 runs in the inning, and there was still only one out. Then it hit me: *This is my inning. I'm the pitcher!* I realized I hadn't technically been taken out of the game and since I was the closer I might be expected out there for the ninth. I'd thrown my uniform in the dirty laundry, so in a panic I found a clubbie and told him I needed my uniform. It was already in the washing machine. So he went to another room and started going through various trunks until he found my spare uniform. I put it on as quickly as I could and ran down the tunnel to the dugout. I got there just as they were sending Scott Service out to pitch. "Good job, Monty, getting us out of that," Tony Muser said. "We're going to turn it over to Scotty now." We won the game 11–7, and I got the win.

* * *

A funny thing happened to the Royals during a four-game stretch at home against the Chicago White Sox and Tampa Bay Rays on Memorial Day weekend in 2016.

This sums it up:

- The Royals came back in three games against the White Sox.
- They won all four games with a late rally, and the rally in each started with one out.
- Friday featured a four-run rally in the seventh inning.
- Saturday featured a seven-run rally in the ninth inning.

Salvador Perez hits the game-winning RBI during the 2014 wild-card game for the Royals, who have been known for their comebacks of late. *(Kansas City Royals)*

- Sunday featured a three-run rally in the eighth inning.
- On Monday the game was tied in the top of the eighth. The Royals scored four in the bottom of the eighth.

Never had a Royals team had as many thrilling come-from-behind wins in team history. It would take watching a lot of baseball to witness a series of games like that one. What we've seen at Kauffman, starting in 2014, is a reason the team can come back late in games. The crowd gets so into it and so loud. It's like a rock concert more than a game. One detail that stands out to me about the come-from-behind wins is the fact that all of the rallies started after the first batter was retired. On the surface, that may not seem too unusual, but as a former pitcher I can attest to the fact that getting the first batter out is the most important.

Going back to the Friday night game, the seventh-inning rally began with Cheslor Cuthbert grounding out before Brett Eibner got things going with his first major league hit, a double. The Royals would go on to score four runs in that inning and win 7–5 after being down by three runs at the start of the bottom of the seventh.

Saturday's game will go down as the most memorable of all the 2016 comeback wins as the Royals were able to score seven runs in the bottom of the ninth for an 8–7 win. That ninth inning started with Sox closer David Robertson retiring Paulo Orlando with a strikeout. What followed was an incredible display of frenzied hitting, and Eibner—in only his second major league game—capped it off by getting the game-winner with his first career walk-off hit. As a closer it's difficult to be in that situation because we're used to going in with the game on the line. It's like you're on the high wire without a net. It made me a better pitcher with more focus and concentration. When it's a 7–1 game, as Robertson found out, that same level of intensity is missing. The tendency for the catcher in a 7–1 game is to put down fastballs. I needed to use all four pitches. It's not long before you have to get into that sense of urgency.

It would have been tough to top Saturday's win in the series finale, but the Royals still managed to erase a 4–2 deficit in the bottom of the eighth inning for a 5–4 win. And yes, the rally started with Whit Merrifield fouling out to start the inning before Lorenzo Cain started the rally by homering to right. To keep the one-out rally theme alive, the Royals began a four-run rally in the eighth inning on Memorial Day after Drew Butera grounded out to start the inning after the Rays had tied the game at 2–2 in the top of the eighth. The Royals eventually won 6–2.

Quick Pitches

I rarely had issues or blowups with umpires. They missed calls, but I hung sliders. There are a couple umpire stories, though, that stand out. We were playing the New York Yankees, and Richie Garcia, who's a great umpire, was behind the plate. Paul O'Neill, my former roommate with the Cincinnati Reds who was a very good and selective hitter, was at the plate in a big situation. With two outs I threw a borderline 3–0 pitch to Paul that Richie called a strike. O'Neill stepped out and let Garcia have it. He was showing up Garcia in front of thousands of people. The next pitch, borderline again, was called strike two. O'Neill again wasn't happy with Richie. I threw the next pitch literally nine inches off the plate, and Garcia called it strike three. Paul went nuts. But it was because Paul had shown him up. If I had thrown it between Paul's neck and ankles and the catcher caught it, it was going to be strike three.

Before Steve Palermo was shot when trying to help out a victim being robbed in 1991, he was a fun, energetic, talkative umpire. He was good for the game. I'll never forget in Seattle late in the 1990 season, we started Chris Codiroli. He gave up only one hit through four and two-thirds innings, but he walked five batters and hit three. He threw 101 pitches. He was effectively wild, but in his wildness, he was bouncing a bunch of pitches to the plate that were catching Palermo. Finally, fed up after getting hit by another ball in the dirt, Steve pulled a new baseball out of his bag and rolled it out to Codiroli.

Steve lives in the Kansas City area, which is great for us because he's an umpire supervisor and is in the press box at Kauffman Stadium for most of our games. He's a tremendous resource for us, a nice luxury to have. I see a lot of umpires from my generation around the league because MLB has a supervisor at every game.

* * *

One of my teammates in 1999 was Scott Pose. Earlier in his career, though, I faced him in a spring training game. He hit a ball down the right-field line—just foul. As he rounded first, Pose was arguing with the umpire about the call. He got in the box, and with the next pitch, I drilled him in the numbers. As he was going to first, I told him, "You want to get on base that badly, here you go." It was quite funny.

* * *

Jose Rosado was a left-handed pitcher for the Royals in the late 1990s. He didn't have great numbers, but he was the club's All-Star in 1997 and '99. I didn't know Rosado very well, but he's part of Royals lore. In August of 1996, we were playing against the Angels in Anaheim. With two outs in the bottom of the fifth inning, Rosado was fielding a pop-up by Todd Green near the dugout. He caught the ball, but he fell in the dugout and got hurt. Manager Bob Boone called on rookie Jaime Bluma, who was making his first major league appearance. Bluma had been an outstanding closer at Wichita State and was a great prospect for the Royals. That night hadn't started with great results for Jaime. Before the game he lost an on-field cow milking contest to fellow rookie pitcher Mike Holtz. Jaime might've felt like an *udder* disappointment in his major league debut, too. With the Royals leading 5–0, Bluma's first batter was Angels second baseman and future Royals announcer Rex Hudler. With a 1–1 count, Hud launched a home run to left-center field for his 14th homer of the season. That was the only run Jaime gave up in his one inning that night. He has joked that "Rex flipped his bat and definitely showboated after hitting it." We held on and beat the Angels 5–3, and I was able to get my 22nd save of the season that night.

* * *

Chris Haney was a finesse lefty who spent parts of seven seasons with the Royals. He was a good teammate, but he didn't enjoy the success that people envisioned for him. For instance, in 1993 he won nine games, but he also lost nine. In 1996 he won 10 games, but he lost 14. But hearing the name Chris Haney today reminds me of another Royals lefty named Jeff Granger.

Granger had been a quarterback at Texas A&M before the Royals selected him in the first round (fifth overall) of the 1993 draft. As a pitcher Granger had a slider that scouts compared to Hall of Fame lefty Steve Carlton. Generally, once the first-round picks sign with the Royals, the club brings them to the stadium for a press conference and then to work out with the team. That was the case for Granger. After the press conference, he headed to the bullpen with the scout who signed him and scouting director Art Stewart and coach Bruce Kison. Our manager, Bob Boone, who'd caught Carlton for many years with the Philadelphia Phillies, wanted to catch Granger in this bullpen session. They finished the workout, and everyone was headed back toward the dugout. Mark Gubicza and I were standing in right field, and Boonie came over to us. We asked him how Granger looked. Boonie said, "I'll be honest with you. I heard comparisons of Steve Carlton, and that's what I was expecting, but I think I just caught Chris Haney." Needless to say, Granger's career didn't turn out like Haney's, let alone Carlton's.

Thinking of Haney reminds me of another story. Jim Pittsley was a tall righty, at about 6'7" and 215 pounds. He was the Royals' first-round pick in 1992 out of high school and spent a few seasons in the major leagues. He happened to be a big cigarette smoker. We were playing a game in Kansas City against the then-Anaheim Angels in June 1998. Phil Nevin was with the Angels, but the year before when he was with Detroit, he went in hard at home plate and had a big collision with Mike Sweeney, who was catching for the Royals. Allegedly, Sweeney and Nevin had made up behind the scenes a day or two after that incident, but not many people knew about it, including our pitchers. So, Nevin was going to get drilled at some point. Sure enough, in the fifth inning against the Angels, Haney drilled Nevin. For all intents and purposes, the issue should be dead. Nevin took out Sweeney; one of our pitchers hit Nevin. Case closed.

The only problem was that while Nevin was getting drilled by Haney, Pittsley was out of sight, taking a smoke break. Pittsley came in the game and faced Nevin in the seventh inning, and what did Pittsley do? He hit Nevin on the first pitch. That started the first of two brawls. (Remember, we're in the seventh inning.) In the eighth inning, Anaheim's pitcher, Rich DeLucia, hit Dean Palmer. Scott Service then hit Darin Erstad in the top of the ninth. In the bottom of the ninth, Anaheim's Mike Holtz hit Jose Offerman. That started the second brawl.

In all, 12 people (seven players, both managers, and three coaches) were ejected that night. A day or two later, both managers—Terry Collins of Anaheim and Tony Muser—were suspended, along with nine players, including Nevin and Pittsley.

* * *

In 1996 I started off the season throwing very well—well enough that I was selected for the All-Star team. Around that time, though, my production tailed off significantly. By September I couldn't get anybody out. My pitching coach and teammates were telling me that my arm angle had dropped down. That's a sign that a pitcher is hurt, but I didn't feel hurt. I felt fine, but the batters were proving otherwise. On September 1 we were in Detroit, and Chris Haney had thrown a really nice game. He had given up only two hits and struck out seven in eight scoreless innings. Manager Bob Boone brought me in to relieve Haney. I threw a pitch to Bobby Higginson that I thought struck him out. Home-plate umpire John Hirschbeck didn't give me the call, and Higginson drilled a base hit on the next pitch. Travis Fryman then came up and hit the second pitch out for a two-run home run that tied the game at 2–2. We won that game 3–2 and improved to 63–75.

But that was the straw that broke the camel's back. Something was wrong. I couldn't keep going out there and giving up leads. We were going to Toronto after that, but before we left, I called general manager Herk Robinson and expressed my frustration. I told him I thought something was wrong with my arm. I already had an MRI, which came back negative. The hitters were telling me otherwise, and my coaches and teammates were telling me about my arm angle, which was causing the ball to flatten out before it got to the plate.

"What do you think?" Herk asked.

"Something's wrong. I think I'm unhealthy."

He said, "Well, we haven't had a 100-loss season yet, and I don't want to have one this year. We need you out there."

"Well, if you keep running me out there," I told him, "I can guarantee we're going to lose 100 games."

We hung up and I went to Toronto with the team. Herk called me the next day and said they'd thought about it and decided to let Dr. Steve Joyce, one of our team doctors, scope my shoulder. Two days later Dr. Joyce scoped my shoulder and said, "When you wake up from surgery, if you have a sling on, that's bad news." When I woke up in the bed at St. Luke's Hospital downtown, there was no sling. I was excited. After they released me, my wife, Tina, was driving me home, and I asked her what Dr. Joyce told her. "He said it was worse than he expected," she said.

But I wasn't wearing a sling, so I was excited and thought things were fine until Tina told me that. A couple days later I went for my follow-up. Dr. Joyce started drawing on the table paper. Basically, I had a torn rotator cuff, bone spur, and torn labrum. I was stunned. I asked him about my chances of pitching again. "You have a chance, but it depends on how hard you rehab," he said.

Within a couple of days, I started rehab and worked and worked and worked to get back. The first batter I faced in 1997 was Rafael Palmeiro, and he hit a home run. I obviously wasn't ready. I'm not sure if I rushed or not, but the second half of that season was great. I'm just glad I called Herk that afternoon in Detroit.

* * *

In 1990 we were playing a spring training game against Toronto in Dunedin, Florida. I was a huge Rush fan, and that day I'd purchased the band's brand new CD, *Chronicles*. I immediately opened it and was playing it in my Sony Discman before the game. Typically in spring training, you'd pitch early in the game while each team's starters were in there, so I pitched my inning fairly early and headed to the clubhouse. While I was in there, the clubhouse manager came up to me and said that someone would like to meet me. "Who is it?"

"Geddy Lee."

"Geddy Lee from Rush?"

"Yep."

Sure enough, the clubhouse manager walked out, and in walked this thin guy with long hair, wearing jeans, a T-shirt, Chuck Taylor sneakers, and little round glasses. He said in this cool, soft-spoken voice, "Hey, Jeff, it's really nice to meet you. I'm Geddy Lee." (As if he had to introduce himself.)

We had a great conversation. I came to find out Geddy is a huge baseball fan, especially of the Blue Jays, and he told me that he wanted to meet me because he and his brother had me on their fantasy team and I'd won games for them. Our conversation turned to music, and I told him that I was a big Rush fan. When he questioned me about it, I reached over, picked up my Discman, and showed him that I'd been listening to *Chronicles*.

"You must be a big fan; that came out just a few days ago," he said. Needless to say, we hit it off. "We'll be touring soon, so if you ever want to go to a show, let me know." So we exchanged phone numbers.

Our family was still living in Cincinnati during the offseason, and one night my wife and I had gone out for dinner. When we got home, we checked our answering machine. The voice on the message said, "Hey Jeff, it's Geddy here. We're going to be in Cincinnati next week. Give me a call. I'm at the Hyatt in Pittsburgh. My alias is Hank Greenberg." By the way, that should show how much Geddy enjoys baseball—using the name of Hank Greenberg, who played for Detroit Tigers in the 1930s and '40s. The next week, I took Chris Sabo, Paul O'Neill, and Pat Tabler to the concert in Cincy. We had a blast; it was really cool.

A few years later in 1993, I was selected for the All-Star Game, which was being played in Baltimore at Camden Yards. Geddy sang the Canadian national anthem, and the Royals were opening the second half of the season at Toronto. As it turned out, Tina and I flew to Toronto on the same flight with Geddy. Do you want to know how well-known Geddy Lee is in Canada? We went through customs with him, and it was a VIP experience. He used his clout to get us through without having to wait. "They're with me," he said.

I don't know how many more Rush concerts I attended over the next few years, but it was a lot—probably half a dozen in different cities. One of the times when they were performing in Kansas City, I had a Royals jersey customized for Geddy with his name on the back and the number "2112," which included my uniform number of 21, but 2112 was also the name of one of their albums. He wore it out for his encore.

Geddy had a collection of memorabilia that traveled with him when they toured. It wasn't to show it off. I just think he enjoyed having it with him on the road. A friend and I went to a Rush concert in Milwaukee and went backstage afterward. Geddy was excited to show us some of the memorabilia in his traveling locker.

One huge piece of Geddy's autographed baseball collection can be seen in Kansas City on display at the Negro Leagues Baseball Museum. Normally ballplayers want to be rock stars, but Geddy Lee wanted to be a baseball player.

CHAPTER 8

1994: THE YEAR THAT CHANGED THE ROYALS

It might seem difficult to place the Royals' struggles of the 1990s and into the 2000s on one day, but I think it's safe to say that the immediate possibility of putting another flag on the hill at Kauffman Stadium was immeasurably affected on August 12, 1994. That's the day when baseball's most heated and most pivotal—not to mention professional sports' longest at the time—work stoppage began.

What turned out to be our final game of 1994 was a 2–1 walk-off loss at Anaheim two days earlier. That loss dropped our record to 64–51. At the time, though, we had been on a roll. Although we'd lost four of our previous five games, those five games were coming on the heels of a 14-game winning streak. Heading into the 2017 season, the 14 wins in a row still ranked as the Royals' second-longest winning streak. Any of us from the 1994 club will tell you that we were extremely confident that we'd end up in the postseason that year.

The date of August 12 wasn't an accident. The All-Star Game had been played, and pennant races were heating up, so there was great interest in baseball. From the players' standpoint, we were prepared for a hard battle with the owners, but we felt on August 12 there was time to negotiate and still have postseason baseball. At the end of the day, I don't think either side envisioned that being the end of the season.

The collective bargaining agreement expired on December 31, 1993, so negotiations had begun much earlier than August of 1994. At the heart of the matter in all of this was the owners wanting a salary cap. They unanimously agreed (28–0) to share revenue as long as they could get us to agree on a salary cap. One issue, however, is that Major League Baseball didn't have a commissioner. Fay Vincent had resigned in September 1992, and Bud Selig, who was the owner of the Milwaukee Brewers, was MLB's acting commissioner. That certainly didn't help the situation.

That was the most mentally grueling time of my life because I was the Royals' player representative. So, I was the information source for our players. That meant I spent the time during the strike going to New

York; Washington, D.C.; Orlando; Dallas; and other places around the country where the association would gather for players to get information in person. Remember, we're talking prior to the Internet, so we'd have conference calls. If a player was in one of the cities when we were having a meeting, he'd show up. The calls would range from covering not that much pertinent information to some serious stuff going on where I had to go over very detailed updates. There were some heated discussions in those meetings and conference calls. I still remember some of these calls where I'd say, "If you want to talk privately or you have questions, call me back after the call." I had three or four who'd call back, literally, in tears. One guy was selling furniture at a store, and he told me his wife was going to leave him because she "didn't marry a furniture salesman." He was a younger player. Other guys would talk about cars being repossessed, losing apartments and houses, and so on. They were unfortunate circumstances, but I was their counselor or priest or sounding board—whatever you want to call it.

While I was our team representative, David Cone was the American League player rep. He'd been very involved in the association. As a result of him being more around the clock and being in New York for extended periods of time, he had a lot to offer during our conference calls with the Royals players. He said, "Hey, if anybody needs money, get in touch with me." There was a strike fund set up to help players financially during the work stoppage, but the younger players didn't have one. Since they were on major league rosters, they couldn't go back to Triple A to play during the work stoppage. When Conie found out we had a few guys who needed help, he wrote personal checks to help them get through. He never asked for the money back.

Being our team's rep, I felt like a lightning rod. Numerous times I'd go to the front door, and a news van was in front of my house. Don Fortune was doing afternoon sports radio in Kansas City, the only afternoon sports show at the time, and he was interviewing me about the strike. I said on the air, "I think we have a good chance to get a deal." Talk about being a lightning rod! I heard from the players association about an hour later, asking me what I was talking about.

Major league teams opened spring training with replacement players, but on March 31, 1995, U.S. District Court judge Sonia Sotomayor of New York ruled that the owners had failed. Her ruling stated that since our CBA had expired the owners couldn't implement a salary cap without the union's approval. As a result the union called off the strike, and the owners ended the lockout.

The timing was great for the players. I don't think any player wanted to be the first to cross the picket line, so to speak, but I think dozens of guys would've been tied for second. We were vulnerable at various stages. It's a credit to our leaders and our staff in New York to keep everybody together because some of those meetings and conference calls across the league were not pretty. The decision to end the strike came at a very good time. I know I was ready for it because it just seemed to keep going and going. It turned out to be seven months of hell.

After the strike we all hurried through an abbreviated spring training. Our first game of the 1995 season was on April 26—26 days after Judge Sotomayor's ruling. I'll always remember the emptiness of the ballparks that season. Our first four games were at home against Baltimore and New York. For our first game back, the attendance was 24,170. For the next three games, which were on the weekend against the New York Yankees, our average was less than 15,000. We went to Minnesota after the New York series, and I got my first save of the season in the first game against the Twins in front of 8,862 people. To put that in perspective, the independent minor league team in Kansas City, the T-Bones, have had several crowds of more than 8,862 people. In certain cities there was a very bitter reaction from the fans because the players were the bad guys. That was something we had to work through. By the middle of the '95 season, some fanbases seemed to forget about the strike. In Toronto,

Baltimore, and Cleveland, for instance, we played in front of 40,000 to 47,000. The Blue Jays, Orioles, and Indians were in contention, and winning erased the bad memories.

Our lowest crowd of the season was here in Kansas City against the Boston Red Sox, when only 7,511 came out. The strike compounded matters in Kansas City. The first year of the wild-card was going to be in 1994, and if we didn't win the division that season, we liked our chances of getting the wild-card spot. That left a bitter taste in the mouths of a lot of Royals fans.

Because the effort to get a salary cap had failed, the large-market owners started signing players to huge contracts. They were putting small markets in the rearview mirror. The national television networks need two teams, and it's better for them to have the Red Sox and the Yankees than the Twins and the Royals. It took three or four years to cycle through, but when you go to arbitration, it's based on similar players—not similar salaries. So the Royals had trouble keeping their young stars because the club's revenues couldn't meet expenses, when similar players in New York and Los Angeles were making a lot more money.

In 1990 the Royals had baseball's highest payroll at a little more than $23 million. The lowest payroll belonged to Baltimore at $8 million. That's a decent disparity, but it's not huge. In 1996, the first full season after baseball resumed, the Yankees had the highest payroll at more than $61 million, and the Royals were 24th out of 28 teams at a little less than $20 million. For the 2000 season, the Yankees passed the $100 million mark, and the Atlanta Braves, Los Angeles Dodgers, and Red Sox were all over $90 million.

Within a week of Judge Sotomayor's ruling, on April 5 and April 6, respectively, the Royals announced they'd traded Brian McRae to the Chicago Cubs for Geno Morones and Derek Wallace, and David Cone to the Blue Jays for Tony Medrano, David Sinnes, and Chris Stynes. That was the writing on the wall for the direction the Royals were going to go.

With the death of Mr. Kauffman on August 1, 1993, David Glass was the chairman of the board for the Royals and he had to operate with fiscal responsibility because of the funds left by Mr. Kauffman. It was a perfect (or imperfect) storm because there was a finite amount of money left by Mr. K, and the board controlled everything. The funds were going to run out at some point. We were actually playing under a salary cap structure because the Royals wouldn't be in a position to compensate on the same level that other teams in large-revenue markets were going to do.

If there's one positive for me, it was getting to know current commissioner Rob Manfred during the strike. In 1994 he was outside counsel for the league. He joined Major League Baseball in an official capacity in 1998. It was obvious that he was going to be a big part of baseball because of his knowledge and how he was instrumental in the history of the game going back to that strike.

The 1994 season was, by far, the most frustrating of my career. I think a lot of players from that time could say the same thing. Ending the season in August marked the premature end of many careers. Some of the players who didn't play after 1994 include Bo Jackson, Goose Gossage, and Kent Hrbek. Tony Gwynn ended the season with a .394 batting average, so we'll never know if he could've reached the elusive .400. And the Montreal Expos, who had the best record in baseball in 1994 at 74–40, were in a worse boat than the Royals. They were forced to trade their star players, their attendance plummeted, and they played their last season in Montreal in 2004. As for the Royals, which were also a part of contraction talks, we had a really solid team in 1994. It was disappointing to have things end the way they did.

There's a lot of talk and a lot of conspiracies about the decade or so after the strike. In order to bring back excitement and fans, did the league turn a blind eye to players using performance-enhancing drugs? Were the balls juiced? Did they shrink the strike zone to bring about more offense?

I was close to Mrs. Kauffman. The passing of her and her husband, Ewing—along with labor unrest—led to some dark days for the Royals in the mid-to-late 1990s. *(Jeff Montgomery)*

I'll address the baseballs and the strike zone first. I don't think the balls were "juiced," per se, but I went on a rehab assignment to Omaha, and the balls they were using were different from what we were using in the major leagues. Major League Baseball was using a Rawlings ROA ball, while Triple A was using a Rawlings RO. Those balls felt different because the seams were raised more. As a result a pitcher could get better movement on the ball. I made that observation that season to a couple guys who'd been up and down between the majors and minors, and they agreed that it was easier to throw in the minor leagues. For pitchers who weren't going from the majors to the minors or vice versa, they wouldn't know the difference because they're using the same ball all season. Does that make a big difference? *Yes.* Hitting a baseball is the hardest thing to do in all of sports and it's made harder by pitchers who can put movement on their pitches. Was that difference in the ball intentional to bring more offense in the majors? We'll likely never know. I do feel the strike zone shrunk dramatically. Pre-1994 we could pitch to the corners of the plate and have it called a strike. That went away. I'm not sure if there was a directive from the league, but it went from a pitcher-friendly zone to a hitter-friendly zone. I noticed more difference in the strike zone than I did in the ability of the hitters. The last half of the '90s, the zone seemed to be about the size of a postage stamp.

As far as steroids, there was talk of certain guys, but it wasn't obvious if they were just working hard in the weight room or if they were getting some assistance. Lifting weights was seen as taboo for baseball players for a while. The old-school thought was that players would get bulky and it would hurt their ability to hit.

A group that specialized in athletic training came to spring training to work with us in the early 1990s. We wouldn't put on baseball equipment; we'd put on sweats and head out for conditioning. That brought a lot of injuries to our pitching staff because of the way we were training. We were doing things that weren't conducive to healthy throwing shoulders. Baseball teams throughout the '90s started hiring full-time strength and conditioning coaches. So someone like Mark Gubicza, who used to bring his own weights because we didn't have a weight room, could leave his personal weights behind.

After the strike the combination of the weights, the "steroid era," the smaller strike zone, and the different ball used brought about an enormous change in how the game was played. Home-run totals were going up, and we started seeing chases for home-run records that seemed unbreakable.

I didn't fully realize how rampant steroids and other performance-enhancing drugs were until the Mitchell Report came out in December 2007. The most shocking thing to me about that was the number of pitchers on the list. It seemed to be about half of the list. My assumption, for a pitcher, is if he used PEDs, he'd be working the other way. As a pitcher when you get big and strong, you can lose flexibility and the ability for precise location. Those things go against what I was taught as a pitcher. I always felt you were better off playing long toss and using very light weights for your shoulder. The whole steroid thing went opposite of my belief. I wouldn't have expected any pitchers to be using, but there were some big names on the list, including Roger Clemens, Andy Pettitte, Kevin Brown, and Eric Gagne.

The other aspect of the strike that's sometimes forgotten is that some of the replacement players—about 35 in all—made it to the major leagues after 1995. During spring training in 1997, the Royals sent Michael Tucker and Keith Lockhart to Atlanta for outfielder Jermaine Dye and pitcher Jamie Walker. The thing I remember about that trade was that we were getting a young outfielder who was going to be a home-run guy, but the left-handed pitcher with him was a replacement player during the strike. As the players rep, I had to deal with that. We had 23 other players who were asking me about it and how we were going to handle it. It was a unique situation because the strike had been over for only a couple years, and we were getting one of the few players in baseball currently who'd been a replacement player. We decided to have a team meeting to welcome them and let Jamie talk. It cleared the air, seemingly almost immediately. I think Jamie handled it professionally and was given the chance to explain why he was a replacement player. The other guys understood, I think, that if they'd been in a similar situation, they would've done the same thing.

It's interesting, if not unfortunate, to look back today and see the domino effect around baseball, and certainly in Kansas City, because of the 1994 strike.

CHAPTER 9

FROM THE MINOR LEAGUES TO THE HALL OF FAME

I love this game. That's the ony reason I played. Like a lot of boys, I imagined playing one day for my favorite team. In my case, growing up in Wellston, Ohio, that favorite team was the Cincinnati Reds and the "Big Red Machine." But I don't know that I ever truly thought it would happen.

So imagine my surprise in June 1983, after going to Marshall University on a baseball scholarship and getting my computer science degree, when I received the news. I remember it as if it were yesterday. I was on a golf course with Dad, when Mom comes screaming for us, holding a piece of paper. We were on the green, and she handed me a telegram. I had been drafted in the ninth round *by the Cincinnati Reds*. After the initial shock, there was a naive part of me that probably thought I'd be playing at Riverfront Stadium within a year or two. I reported initially to their team in Billings, Montana, and began to work through their system. Five years later my dream became a reality.

Making it to the major leagues almost didn't happen for me, but there were a few pivotal moments that helped me. I was playing winter ball for Royals pitching coach Frank Funk in Puerto Rico in 1986. I had my degree in computer science, and Tina had her degree in business. So we had some serious discussions of whether to continue to chase the dream of playing in the major leagues or to put our college degrees to work. At that point I hadn't been called up and I felt there were players who didn't have near the resume that I had on the field, statistically speaking, and were being put on the major league roster. Adding to that, our first child was born in September, and either Tina or I needed a "real" job to make "real" money to support our young family.

Before I went to winter ball, I spoke with Chief Bender, the Reds' director of their farm system, and told him that if I was going to continue playing, I had to be compensated. We talked about it some more before I told him that I needed three times what I was making in Triple A. "That's not a doable number," he said.

"That makes my decision for me," I said. "I'm not going to winter ball. I'm going to start a career with my computer science degree."

He called me back later and said the Reds wanted me to keep playing, so I'd have a new contract in December. After playing in Puerto Rico, I got a new contract in December, but it was the standard rate, not the amount Chief and I talked about. So I called him and asked about it. Suddenly, he had amnesia. "I would've never agreed to that," he said.

At that point I started sending out resumes and interviewed with the Hershey Chocolate Company as a systems analyst, which is how I was going to use my degree. I went through a couple interviews and reached a point in late January or early February where they were checking references. Evidently, they called Chief for a reference. As soon as he hung up with them, Chief called me and asked, "What's the meaning of this? How can you start a job with Hershey when spring training starts in a few weeks?"

"I'm not going to spring training," I said. "Evidently you acquired amnesia about my contract, and it's time for me to walk away." We talked for a few more minutes, and after he said they couldn't pay me more, he asked what it would take for me to play another year.

If I could get on the major league 40-man roster, even playing in the minor leagues, it would be huge. As a roster player, even playing in the minor leagues, I would've gotten $40,000 a year. As a non-roster player in the minor leagues, it was $1,200 a month for only the months we played. So I asked Chief, "How about an invitation to major league spring training?"

Chief agreed to it, though I'd be a non-roster invitee. Either way, that was an enormous step for my career and probably helped me end up in the major leagues later that season. So, even though I never used my degree for a job, it got me in the door with the major leagues.

After five years in the minor leagues, the Reds called me up in July 1987. My debut came a couple days later on Saturday, August 1, 1987, at Riverfront Stadium. We thought there was a chance I might pitch, so my parents had come to the game. Fortunately or unfortunately, the San Francisco Giants were blowing us out. The Giants jumped on our starter, Bill Gullickson, early in the game. They took a 4–0 lead through the first three innings. They didn't score in the fourth but made up for it with three in the fifth and led 7–0. In the sixth inning, manager Pete Rose brought me in for my major league debut, replacing Bill Scherrer, who'd come in for Gully in the fifth. Running onto that field at the only place I'd ever seen a major league game was a special moment. In spite of whatever nerves I may have been feeling, I threw okay for two innings. I walked a couple and gave up a hit to Jeffrey Leonard, but I didn't allow a run.

The next day the game was closer. The crowd of more than 44,000 saw the Reds tie the game at 4–4 in the bottom of the eighth. The game went into extra innings. Since I pitched the day before and hadn't pitched yet on this hot Sunday afternoon, my dad figured I wouldn't be pitching this day, so he decided he wanted to beat the traffic out of downtown Cincinnati, and he and my mom left. They were surprised and a little disappointed in themselves when they heard radio broadcasters Marty Brennaman and Joe Nuxhall say I was coming in for the top of the 11th inning. I had a fairly clean inning of work. After walking Chili Davis with two outs, I struck out Bob Melvin. In the bottom of the 11th inning, Eric Davis hit the first pitch he saw from Jeff Robinson out of the park for a walk-off home run and my first major league win.

We then went to the West Coast and got swept in San Francisco. After one of the games at Candlestick Park, I was going to meet my cousin for dinner, so I hurried to the shower to get out of there. Pete came in and started showering. It was just the two of us, and he told me he was going to start me Thursday night in Los Angeles against the Dodgers, but he wasn't going to announce it until Wednesday. So I didn't say anything to anyone, per Pete's request. That was great news, though, because I had been a starter in the minor leagues.

As promised, I started the game against Bob Welch, who was pitching for the Dodgers. My starting debut didn't go well at all. I gave up eight hits and five runs in five innings. The Dodgers led 5–1 when I came out of the game. After that night Pete used me sparingly out of the bullpen in mop-up games for the rest of the season. In fact, I pitched only 10 more times, and eight of those games were losses for the team. The Reds "sent" me down for a day or two in August—though I didn't actually go to the minor leagues—so they could make a roster move for playoff eligibility. I was an afterthought.

There are a couple postscripts to that story. The next February is when the Reds traded me to Kansas City. About two years after I was traded and establishing myself with the Royals, I was still living in Cincinnati during the offseason. I went to a workout with Doug Bair at Northern Kentucky University. Murray Cook, the general manager for the Reds, was there to watch Doug. After we finished we went to lunch, and I asked Murray why they traded me. Again, I was elated to be in Kansas City, but I was curious about the trade. He said that Pete had given him a list of a half-dozen players and said, "Trade them or release them. It doesn't matter. These guys will never play for me." I was one of those six.

The second addendum to my abbreviated time with Pete and the Reds in 1987 could be an aha moment for the conspiracy theorists. Three or four years later, all of Pete's gambling information started coming out. I was informed that the game I started against the Dodgers—my only major league start—was one that, allegedly, Pete had bet on us to win. I didn't pitch well. We didn't win, and I ended up in the doghouse.

During the offseason after my debut with the Reds, I picked up the *Cincinnati Enquirer* in November of 1987 and read that Ted Power and infielder Kurt Stillwell, who was in my 1983 draft class for Cincinnati, had been traded to the Royals for Danny Jackson and Angel Salazar. When I told Tina that Ted, who incidentally went to college at Kansas State, had been traded to Kansas City, she facetiously quipped, "I really hope they enjoy *Kansas*."

About three months later, on February 15, 1988, Chief Bender called and said I'd been traded to the Royals for Van Snider. Based on my experience in 1987 with the Reds, the trade seemed like a great situation for me because the Royals were three years removed from winning the World Series and they were really good. In spite of that, I'd heard of only a handful of players, so I felt confident about the opportunity coming here. After hanging up with Chief Bender, I told Tina, "I have good news and bad news. The good news is that I've been traded to an organization where I have a good chance of being in the major leagues." She thought that was great and then asked for the bad news. "It's the Kansas City Royals."

"Oh, no," she replied. "I should've never said that about Kansas when Power was traded there."

With all that I had gone through—from nearly walking away to going to the minor leagues immediately with the Royals to then seeing the club bring in Mark Davis—I never could've imagined my career going the way it did. I could not have scripted becoming one of the top closers in Royals history. There's no way I remotely thought about having saves numbers close to Dan Quisenberry.

After shoulder surgery ended my 1996 season, I worked hard to get back to normal in 1997. The first batter I faced was Rafael Palmeiro, who hit a home run. It was obvious I wasn't ready to pitch at that level. Spring training is great because you can get your reps. At the start of the season, everyone turns it up a notch from a seven to 10 for regular games. My volume was already at 10 in spring training, so I couldn't turn it up any more. As much as I wanted it to be and as hard as I tried to make it, it just wasn't there.

I struggled for several weeks before deciding in the middle of April that it was time to retire. We were playing the Texas Rangers in mid-April, and I faced Dean Palmer, who later played for the Royals. I threw my best fastball and I think the velocity was 93 miles an hour. It was on

Though getting traded from Cincinnati was tough initially, I definitely found a great home with the Kansas City Royals. *(Jeff Montgomery)*

the inside part of the plate, and Dean turned on it and hit it about 35 rows into the general admission seats. I went home that night and told Tina that I was going to retire. As she has been throughout the entire time we've known each other, she was supportive.

I went to the ballpark the next day and I talked to pitching coach Bruce Kison and manager Bob Boone in the trainer's room with trainer Nick Swartz. I told them I felt I wanted to retire. I couldn't get strong and healthy and ready. They basically said no, we're not going to let you retire. Nick, who was there with me during the entire shoulder rehab and worked so hard to get me healthy, didn't want me to hang it up. Boonie said he wanted me to consider turning to the knuckleball because he'd seen it and thought it was pretty good. So, they shut me down for two weeks. They brought me back in early May, and I continued pitching, but I still wasn't back to 100 percent. Midway through July I had only three saves. We were in Oakland for a series in mid-July, and I went out to the ballpark to throw early hitting to Jermaine Dye and Johnny Damon. It was 2:00 in the afternoon, so there was no radar gun and no one in the stands. It was just those guys in the cage and me on the mound. I threw mainly fastballs at first and then I went to my best pitch, the slider. For the first time since I hurt my shoulder a year earlier, my slider had bite to it. It was back. I realized that day that it probably would've been back sooner, but I came back from shoulder surgery throwing harder than I ever had. That wasn't good for me because I was muscling the ball more. That afternoon in Oakland, I wasn't worried about a radar gun; I was just throwing the ball. It was natural. That's the moment it clicked for me that I needed to let it all happen and not try to force it.

That night, I came in for the bottom of the eighth inning, and the second pitch I threw to the first batter, Mark McGwire, went out for a home run to dead center. Other than that 1–0 pitch, everything else was good. From that point on in 1997, I gave up only two runs in 25 outings. That was a far cry from the 22 runs I'd given up in my first 30 appearances that season.

I went from almost becoming a knuckleballer to getting my season back on track after that afternoon session in Oakland.

Two years later, in 1999, it finally was time to retire. There wasn't a moment when it hit me that it was time; it was an ongoing struggle through the season. After hurting my hip in spring training that year and having a dead arm from overuse, I couldn't get it going. I wasn't going to quit during the season, but I wanted it to be over. In my experience, going into games, you'd hear the crowd cheering, but once you got the ball, you didn't hear any of that. When I was struggling, I could hear the boos and the dissatisfaction from fans. I always said the hitters and my wife would let me know when it was time. The hitters let me know from my lack of performance. Tina was honest with me and said, "You don't need to go through this anymore."

Coincidentally, Palmer, who was one of the hitters who made me think I was done in 1997, was one of the last batters I faced when I did retire in 1999. We were playing host to the Detroit Tigers for a weekend series to wrap up the season. We were trailing 4–2 Saturday when I came out with two on and one out in the top of the ninth. Dean was the first batter I faced. This time I struck him out on three pitches. I then got Damion Easley to ground out, which ended the inning. We scored a run in the bottom of the inning but lost 4–3.

Sunday's weather was miserable, so neither team took batting practice on the field. I saw Dean in the lobby at Kauffman Stadium as both of us were headed down to the clubhouse. He said, "I heard you're going to retire. Why?" I told him about my hip and the frustration of being ineffective that season, and he said, "Your slider last night was as good as I've ever seen it." That was nice of him to say, but I was ready to leave because I wasn't as good consistently as a valuable major league player needs to be. I just couldn't generate that push that I needed for that level. (Little did I realize that I'd be getting a new hip 15 years later.) You get spoiled as a player when you have success because you create a level of expectation for everyone around you—the manager, players, fans. More importantly, inside your heart and mind, that level exists. You expect to play above that level and when you don't it's frustrating. As I mentioned earlier in the book, George Brett was our best player when he retired, but he wasn't "George Brett best." Every player has that built-in level that he uses as his barometer. I experience that even now outside of baseball. There's a competitiveness inside all athletes that's a motivating factor. I think that's why some guys perform above their talent. It's why I was able to perform at the major league level as a ninth-round pick instead of a first-round pick. There was never a point in the 1999 season when I sensed I'd get back to that level. Midway through the season, it became evident that it wasn't going to happen.

Since that Sunday's game was inconsequential, they called it late that morning. All the guys then came around in the clubhouse and congratulated me. Some guys asked me to sign baseballs or equipment. Everything was fine. I took off my uniform, threw it into the dirty clothes pile, and went to the shower. That's when it hit me that it was over. I stood there and cried for about 20 minutes. Once that was out of my system, I was over it. I decided to get dressed and get on with my life. That's the last time I ever thought about walking away from baseball. I'd milked every ounce of baseball out of my body, and it was time to move on. The Chiefs were on the road that day. Since the game was rained out, Tina invited a bunch of friends to the house to watch the Chiefs. That was it.

The next spring a few teams called to see if I was *really* retired. One of those calls came from my old coach, Bruce Kison, who was with the Baltimore Orioles. "We can guarantee you a spot in the bullpen if you show up," he said. It was humbling that he called, but it wasn't remotely tempting. I hadn't picked up a baseball since October and I didn't have any plans to pick one up. My daughter, Ashleigh, was a freshman in high school. I was gearing up to coach the little league team of my son, Connor. I'd missed a lot of the events for our kids. Tina had been both mother and father for long enough. It was time to be around the house. That made it easy. I never looked back.

In early 2003 I found out I had been elected to the Royals Hall of Fame. Besides the Baseball Hall of Fame in Cooperstown, New York, being selected for your team's Hall of Fame is one of the highest honors a player can receive. Being elected to the Royals Hall of Fame was the payoff for the work of so many people around me. I was rarely ever the best player on any team I played on, but I was given opportunities to go to the next level. I definitely was a long shot for the Royals Hall of Fame, but there were enough good people involved in my progression that allowed it to happen.

For me the selection was a culmination of my baseball life. If you take all things you do, even going back to little league, minor leagues, and then major leagues and put it all together, that's what I remember feeling when they told me I'd been elected. It was a finishing moment to my baseball life. It was a proud moment for my family, particularly my mom and dad, who'd given me tremendous opportunities throughout my amateur baseball career and helped me get to college.

The ceremony was on Saturday, August 2. They brought me onto the field at Kauffman Stadium on the back of this convertible. That's when the sense of the moment first hit. The Royals were having a really good season and seemed destined for the playoffs, so there were about 35,000 people there giving me a standing ovation. It was a very overwhelming moment. You can't prepare yourself for it.

It was a very enjoyable day highlighted by family and friends who were there. My college coach, Jack Cook, and pitching coach, Greg Rowsey, came in for it, as did my high school coach, Pat Hendershott, plus tons of family and friends. The night before Tina threw a party for me, and we had about 400 people there. It was a tremendous celebration.

The Royals told me I had four minutes for the speech. Knowing the players had a game to play in a really good season, I had a four-minute speech, but, unfortunately, it took me about eight minutes to deliver it. Not because of emotions but because of the echo in the stadium. That threw me a curve. The highlight was throwing the first pitch. I threw a lot of last pitches at Kauffman Stadium, but that's the only first pitch I ever threw there. The catcher was my dad, which made it even more special. That's a night and an experience I'll never forget.

CHAPTER 10
A VIEW FROM THE BOOTH

Before my baseball career ended, I was thinking about what I was going to do in my next phase of life. With my computer science degree, I felt comfortable that I'd be doing something with that. In 1997 I became a shareholder at Union Broadcasting, which has several radio stations, including WHB in Kansas City. Although I'm occasionally on the air as a baseball analyst, my main job is working as Union's vice president of digital media. Basically, I'm in charge of the station's website and the digital content.

My radio work at WHB is what eventually got me on television. Mike Swanson, the Royals' vice president of broadcasting and communications, called me in 2009 and asked if he could put my name in the hat with FOX Sports to be an analyst on the TV broadcasts on an as-needed basis. I knew all the people on the TV side, including producer Kevin Shank, so I told Swanee that'd be great. In December I talked with someone from FOX, but there wasn't any type of job offer. Weeks went by without any word. And then months. The season started and still no word. I figured they didn't need any help.

In May of 2010, Kevin called and asked if I still had an interest in doing TV. He said they wanted to start working me into games. "When can you start?" he asked.

"When are you thinking?"

"Today at 3." We talked for a few more minutes, he told me to wear a coat and tie, and then I headed to the ballpark. That was it. There were no classes or anything formal. They just threw me into the fire. I ended up doing 15 or 20 games that season. I've always described it like going out to the Kansas Speedway, being handed keys to a car, and being told to drive around the track at 200 miles an hour. At first you'll likely be timid or may drive recklessly. The more and more you're in that car driving 200 miles an hour, the more comfortable you'll become. Well, the more times you're in front of the camera, the easier it gets. A FOX associate told me during my first season that it'd take about 500 shows before

To me broadcasting is the second best job in baseball—right behind playing.
(Kansas City Royals)

I was comfortable. He was right. We had former pitcher Bruce Chen on for a few games in 2015. Being around him reminded me how tough and nerve-wracking this job is at first. Bruce was asking the same questions I'd asked years earlier. At one point he told me, "This is way harder than pitching!" Broadcasting is a very fluid position, and you have to think on your feet. It's probably the second best job in baseball.

Paul Splittorff was a great announcer, and I knew he had some health issues, but I didn't know the extent. He had an issue with his voice, but publicly he said it was some type of virus. On Opening Day 2011, I was doing the pregame and postgame show at the Rivals Bar inside Kauffman Stadium. I was on with Splitt and host Joel Goldberg. I think they were getting Splitt to teach me how to do this job. We were walking from Rivals toward the press box when I noticed Splitt was limping. "You have a hitch in your giddy-up, Splitt?"

"Oh, I was on the treadmill too long today," he said.

In reality, he had a melanoma on his calf, which we found out about a little more than six weeks later when he died on May 25 of complications from melanoma and oral cancer. (Sady and coincidentally, it was melanoma that took Splitt's good friend and longtime radio broadcaster Fred White almost two years to the day after on May 15, 2013.) I don't know that Splitt was trying to hide the cancer or if that was Splitt not wanting any extra attention. The Royals were in Baltimore for a three-game series starting on May 24, and I got a call from someone at one of the local TV stations asking if I'd heard anything about Splitt. I hadn't, but this reporter told me that Splitt was very ill and didn't have time to leave. Sadly, it was an accurate story, as he died the next day.

Splitt's playing career ended before I made it to the major leagues, but he was the TV analyst and did some fill-in radio when I was playing. He was very good on the air. As a player, there was a very significant level of trust with Splitt. I could always talk with him about anything, knowing that it wasn't going to end up on a broadcast.

Much like his playing career, Splitt worked hard to become the best broadcaster he could be. Actually, the best advice I've ever received in broadcasting was from Splitt. "As a player you give up a home run to lose a game and you don't sleep at night," he said. "As a broadcaster you'll make a mistake, but never go back to your hotel or home and worry about it. Don't dwell on mistakes. As a player your performance is based on preparation, and the same is true as a broadcaster." That gave me tremendous perspective. He saw so many broadcasters in all sports show up unprepared. Those were the guys who eventually didn't make it. It becomes apparent when people around you have to carry the load.

Joel Goldberg is another great partner and he's really good on television. He has a phenomenal ability to multitask. Viewers don't see him reading the opening billboard for the show while he's checking stats on his iPad at the same time. I'm lucky to work with someone like Joel, who's been in this business for a while and is a great partner. If I had something that I felt was important to say, Joel would set me up. He was instrumental in my successful transition from former player to broadcaster. Most former players are thrown into a much hotter fire going from the field to the booth.

In those first couple years, we did a lot of pregame prepping. Now we usually spend about 20 to 30 minutes together before a show, but we have so much information available that we could show up five minutes before and we'd probably be fine. We've done more than a thousand shows together so we know each other well enough that we know what to expect with each other. In the beginning we had to spend more time together because I wasn't experienced.

We're like The Odd Couple, though. I have the old baseball mentality that if you're five minutes early, you're late. So, for a 6:30 airtime, I'm on the set by 6:10. Joel oftentimes is really late. Sometimes it's out of his control—usually not, at least before a game. After the game is a different story. When the Royals win and he does his postgame interview on the field with a player, he throws it to Ryan Lefebvre and Rex Hudler, who wrap up the broadcast. Meanwhile, Joel's hustling out to the set, which is next to the Royals Hall of Fame building. The timeframe is so short that our postgame producer tells me how we're going to open the postgame show in case Joel isn't out there in time. Since it's live TV with set commercial breaks, there's not an opportunity for: "Hey, wait a minute, we're not ready." So, as the producer is telling me how we're going to open the show and with what highlights, I'm scrambling to write it down. With literally just seconds to spare, Joel usually gets to the set, dripping wet from sweat and a "Salvy Splash" in time to insert his earpiece and hear, "Okay, Joel, we have 45 seconds." Five seconds before we go on, he's ready. Knock on wood; he's never missed the open, so I've never had to open. Five years ago if they were getting me ready to open the show, I'd tell them to cancel it. Now, I think I'd be okay to open it if absolutely necessary. It's funny what driving that car around the track more than 500 times at 200 miles an hour can do.

Ryan Lefebvre came to Kansas City in my worst year as a player—1999, my last season. He came at a difficult time because he was the replacement for longtime radio broadcaster Fred White. I wouldn't wish that situation on anyone. It was a very difficult transition for Ryan to start working with Denny Matthews, who's legendary, and Ryan was replacing Fred, who also was legendary. For Kansas City fans listening to the Royals on radio meant simply "Denny and Fred" or "Fred and Denny" for 25 years. But Denny and Fred made Ryan feel welcomed, and his personality is such that he doesn't have an ego, and he's a calming influence to everyone around him.

I got to know Ryan while I was playing, which was beneficial for me, even though there was no way to guess that we'd be working together one day on the television broadcasts. In recent years Ryan has made the transition from almost exclusive work on radio to almost exclusive work on TV with limited time on radio.

During a beautiful day at Kauffman Stadium, I broadcast with my great partner, Joel Goldberg. I call us "The Odd Couple." *(FOX Sports Kansas City)*

Ryan has great knowledge of the game after growing up around it at the major league level with his dad, Jim Lefebvre, who is a former player, coach, and manager. Ryan played collegiately at the University of Minnesota and then briefly in the Cleveland Indians organization. That helps to give him a nice perspective on the game overall and on moments in each game. Ryan is as prepared as he can get each night, which is a trait that I'm guessing he honed a little by working with Splitt.

Similarly to Ryan, Rex Hudler joined the Royals TV broadcasts in less-than-perfect circumstances. He was filling the shoes of a guy—Frank White—who has a statue at the stadium and whose No. 20 is hanging on the Hall of Fame building. That's not easy, especially considering his style is completely opposite of Frank's. It was tough on him that first year, but everyone on our broadcast team did all we could to help him through it. I think he struggled with some of the negative criticism, but there was going to be negativity regardless of his style simply because of who he was replacing. Now he's one of the most popular members of our team.

Adding to some of that early criticism is that Hud came in without any type of Royal blue blood flowing through his veins. His lack of familiarity was a huge hurdle to overcome, but he's learned. He's improved in regards to his knowledge of the organization. Fortunately, the team has improved on the field as he's learned more of the history. He came in when the team was still in the early stages of getting to the top. Now the popularity of the TV broadcasts, I think, has helped him grow on people. Of the people who were not fans of Hud in the beginning, they may never be happy with him, but there are younger viewers who are excited about him. Ultimately, the Royals attracted some younger viewers.

People often ask me if Rex is being a showman with his unique phrases, such as "driving the bus," "pilot to bombardier," "sneaking a piece of cheese past a hungry rat," "check, please," and, of course, when he called the moon a "beautiful planet." The guy you hear on the broadcasts is the real Rex. He's the same off the set as he is on the set. He's sentimental, caring. He loves people, he's passionate about this game, and he quickly fell in love with the Kansas City area.

That said, Joel and I wear earpieces during the broadcasts, and we hear everything that's said—even things that don't go out over the air. I think at least one point in every game there's a time when Joel and I start looking at each other and laughing or shake our heads at either something that was said over the air or something that was off the air between Hud and the truck. We are fortunate to be entertained nightly. We have a lot of fun with it. Here are two of my favorites.

We were in Chicago playing the White Sox at U.S. Cellular. There, Joel and I are in the TV booth on an elevated row behind Ryan and Rex.

Hud was talking about White Sox manager Robin Ventura and how the season hadn't gone the way he'd hoped it'd go. Hud said, "Robin Ventura's gonna have to go after those noassitol pills, get something for his stomach." Hud meant antacid pills. Not many people knew what "no-ass-at-all" pills were. However, I'd heard that occasionally in a clubhouse, so I started laughing. Nobody knew why. Joel whispered to me, wanting to see what was so funny. After I explained it, he started laughing. Eventually Ryan said on the air, "Hud, what kind of pills were those?" When Rex saw me laughing, he had a blank look on his face like *what did I just say?* Then he realized and started laughing. There was what seemed about two minutes of silence on the air because we couldn't stop laughing.

Another time, we were in New York at Yankee Stadium and while Hud and Ryan were talking about Salvador Perez, Hud said, "Can you imagine Salvy in Yankee pinstripes? Sal, being one of the most popular players, he's huge in K.C. and he'd be bigger in New York." Of course, any self-respecting Royals fan can't stand the Yankees, but Rex only meant that Salvy would be ridiculously famous if he was in the nation's largest city. Ryan, who seemed to be caught off guard, said, "No, Hud, I can't imagine him in Yankee pinstripes." Hud tried backpedaling and saying something about Salvy wearing a pinstripe suit to accept an award, but it was too late. There's a glass partition separating the TV booth from where we were sitting on the press side, and Hud was signaling to me to go in and get on the air with them to help him out. There was no way.

Because of the time we spend together with the TV and radio broadcasters during a season, we all look at each other as teammates. That includes "the guys in the truck." We have a very good team, especially behind the scenes. Broadcasters from other teams tell us on a regular basis how fortunate we are in Kansas City to have such a cohesive broadcast unit. We agree; we're spoiled. What we have is the norm for us, but it's not the norm around Major League Baseball. Our crew does so much that no one ever sees or could imagine.

We have a home crew and then a core group of personnel that travels with us. At home we have camera operators, a producer for pregame and postgame, a producer for the game broadcast, associate producers, and a director. They're remarkable.

Of all the broadcasts, perhaps the most enduring memory is from a road contest in Boston. During my career as a player in the American League, I would have made roughly 25 trips to Boston to play baseball against the Red Sox. I have several fond memories from those road trips to one of my favorite cities in our great country. None of the trips I made to Boston as a player will ever leave such a lasting memory as the trip I made in April 2013.

On Friday morning the 19th, Tina and I were to fly to Boston for me to work the series for FOX Sports. Earlier that week on Monday the 15th, two bombs went off near the finish line of the Boston Marathon. Three people were killed, and hundreds were seriously wounded. On Friday we awoke to news that authorities had been working throughout the night after developments in the manhunt for the Boston Marathon bombers had intensified. We initially thought our chances of getting to Boston that day were very slim but later learned our flight was scheduled to depart on time. On the way to the airport, we both received numerous messages from friends wondering if we were still going to make the trip. Most assumed we would never make it.

Upon our arrival at the Boston airport, we were surprised to learn that taxi service was available and we were going to be able to make it from the airport to our hotel through a city that was on lockdown. We were prepared for a long stay at the airport until the lockdown was lifted. Instead we made it in record time as there was virtually no traffic. As we got near the hotel, which was very close to the scene of the bombings, we saw every major news station set up and covering the events.

When we arrived at the team hotel, we saw several of the Royals players, coaches, and media members in the lobby awaiting word on whether

It's not quite as thrilling as when I played, but I enjoy being connected to the game and the Royals through my broadcast work. *(Kansas City Royals)*

or not there would be Friday night baseball. As it turned out there was no game on Friday night, but a much more significant event occurred later that evening when the second bombing suspect was apprehended. We were at Daisy Buchanan's, an old bar near the team hotel that was a popular spot for professional athletes, watching the events unfold on TV. It was at that time when the city of Boston began its celebration. Normally a city-wide celebration follows the Boston Marathon on Patriots' Day each spring in Boston, but this celebration, which was delayed by more than five days, will be one that no Bostonian will ever forget.

On Saturday there was baseball, but before the seemingly meaningless game started, there was an on-field ceremony that brought tears to almost everyone in attendance when the victims were honored, and those who responded to assist the injured were recognized. It was truly one of the most vivid moments any American could experience and certainly one that I will never forget.

AFTERWORD
BLUE PAIN TO
BLUE REIGN

If you watch the television broadcasts of our games, at least a couple times during each series, you'll hear the name David Holtzman or "Holtzy." He's an associate producer, but a couple years before joining our FOX broadcasts, Holtzy was in the Royals media relations department. He was around the club during Dayton Moore's early years and now he's seen the resurgence as a member of our broadcast team. Shortly after the 2016 season, Holtzy penned the following poem about how far this organization has come.

"Transformation is a process, and as life happens, there are tons of ups and downs. It's a journey of discovery—there are moments on mountaintops and moments in deep valleys of despair." —*Rick Warren*

Back during the dark times, there was no light.
No joy in the stands, just a team not quite right.

These were times of laughter and mocking,
Shared sadly and simply by media who wouldn't stop talking.

The jokes were many, and the insults flew.
The fans wore bags, as the players' successes were few.

The list is extensive and reaches as tall as mountains.
Bad news for the team in the shadow of fountains.

Was it July 4th, a Fireworks Friday, or a big win?
Nope. Just a walk from a boneheaded slugger named Quinn.

Harvey couldn't compete in that wrestling match.
The tarp swallowed him whole in an ugly flash.

MacDougal had an easy play at the plate in Seattle,
But the ball seemingly was filled with helium as we lost the battle.

Affeldt never saw that rosin bag in the NYC.
And a win disappeared in a white puff of agony.

Big Ken returns to our list with a bang and a thud.
A throw home doesn't quite get there with Grimsley, his bud.

The losing streak is over as Ambres moves toward the line.
And he dropped it; yes, he did, and the streak is still fine.

Eduardo Villacis, not much more to say.
He was K.C.'s sacrificial lamb that day.

The best of the best gathered at PNC.
Is that really Redman representing K.C.?

Hey, it's time to bring Harvey back to get clowned.
When Stairs literally "hit the cutoff man" and he fell to the ground.

And Ambres returns to our list as K.C. fans cry.
He and Long in the outfield? One surely will catch that fly.

A time for celebration 20 years in the making,
But 1985 reunion weekend washed out and left fans aching.

How about some fire in the dugout on a September night?
Buck and Runelvys separated after a several-punches fight.

Let's say they call it the Windy City for a reason.
Why else would Kerry climb the wall in Chicago that season?

Hey Esteban, who needed sunglasses on the plane,
    but not on the field?
I hope eventually that black eye was healed.

Then one day halfway through another century-defeating season,
A man named Moore gave optimistic fans a reason.

A reason for hope and a reason for belief.
The process was here; K.C. had a new chief.

They would build from within with toughness and smarts.
A championship organization with really big hearts.

A cast was assembled and would scour the world.
No one would rest until another pennant was unfurled.

J.J., Dean, Rene, Scott, Gene, and the like,
Joined the quest on this long, but rewarding hike.

The mountain was steep and fraught with danger.
There was no guarantee that first rounder was a game-changer.

And sure, there were many failures along the way.
Too many to name, but it's time for nice things to say.

Billy and Gordo could serve as the base.
Gil was brought in to lead the staff as the ace.

And while the results produced initially were hard to watch,
A culture was forming as talent rose on the farm notch by notch.

Hoch, Perez, Moose from SoCal, and then the big man at first.
Winning minor league titles together provided a thirst.

Zack developed into the best pitcher in ball.
He was then shipped to "Brew Country" for quite the haul.

The All-Star extravaganza visited town.
And K.C.'s love of baseball was once again found.

Then a trade to signal that it was time to win.
Arms and attitudes from the Rays to serve as the linchpin.

In 2013, a huge step taken as September was meaningful.
No postseason ball, but the boys had successfully ridden the bull.

The following season would start with promise as any other.
Everyone was engaged as the spring turned to summer.

When they danced with the Tigers at the top of the charts,
The loyal fans felt much warming in their hearts.

July turned to August, the division chances were fading.
Some were upset at the complete lack of trading.

But an impassioned Raul would not let them quit.
He believed in something special and saw historic grit.

And in the house of Robinson's prior misguided leap,
J-Guts, Holly, and Salvy provided memories to keep.

The playoffs were a reality, it was time already.
The anthem played on repeat, it said "We Ready."

Four days later a gathering 29 years in the making,
Early the green-clad men from Oakland left us shaking.

Moss went deep not once, but twice.
The second off "Ace" came after Ned rolled the dice.

Lester up four with six outs to go?
Most would give in, but The K remained aglow.

A track meet led by Rusty proceeded to break out.
And very quickly, it seemed, the crowd began to shout.

More running in the ninth down by one run.
Aoki sac fly and the Athletics lead was none.

When old friend Alberto seemingly daggered the cause,
Hosmer stepped to the plate in the bottom with staggering applause.

Eric's three-bagger increased the tension.
Colon's chopper was then beyond comprehension.

Another swipe and then Salvy was ready for his signature time.
A reach, a connection, and a sprint; a moment for a lifetime.

A life-altering night had come to an end.
And after a party, a quick turnaround to attend.

Flying to Cali for a matchup with the top seed.
No time to stop or for the momentum to recede.

Big pitches were made, and the gloves were performing.
An unwavering attitude had begun forming.

And in the end, a couple of powerful swings.
By those first rounders sent us home like kings.

The third one seemed easier, even Billy swiped a bag.
And when it was over, we were four wins from the flag.

The Chessmaster and the Dunce is how the next was perceived.
But in the end, it would be those orange birds that grieved.

More late-inning wonder and some Lorenzo magic.
The Charm City's attitude was somewhere near tragic.

Two more tight ones at home did follow.
How in the heck did Moose catch that ball? Oh!

And when that throw nestled snuggly in Hosmer's glove,
The fans and the team shared feelings of unmistakable love.

Buying drinks for the multitude down at the P&L,
Was impossible not to feel the ground swell.

The Fall Classic would go the full seven.
At times it certainly seemed we'd be taken to heaven.

Infante's blast, the bullpen's dominance.
Yordano's flair will lead us to prominence.

But, oh, that "Bum" in orange and black.
With the three-quarter delivery and devastating yak.

Questions abound when the Panda pulled in that pop fly.
The answers we'd learn in 12 months exactly why.

An offseason came next with focus and stewing.
A championship pedigree was quickly renewing.

Spring came again not a moment too soon.
The path was remarkably clear by as early as June.

Unfinished business was a statement fairly often.
Day in and day out, no one's passion would soften.

July brought a twirler with some unusual hair.
His shimmies and shakes carried oodles of flair.

A switch hitter came next with a discerning eye.
He completed the lineup, and the boys were ready to fly.

By the ninth month, the only question remained,
Was home-field advantage there to be gained?

A final five victories provided the answer.
The K would be the locale for a likely advancer.

The first foe perhaps proved the most severe.
The Houston boys had another gutsy gear.

Once again, the blue found a familiar hill to climb.
Without another mad rally, K.C. was looking at more downtime.

It started quite simply with a single to left.
Ten batters later we were all out of breath.

In the middle of the madness, a grounder was struck.
A bouncer toward the middle that would bring much good luck.

The result of the frame left the locals in silent shock.
They didn't know that this K.C. group was a valuable stock.

A stock that was building for years in worth,
Through wins, losses, and an organization's rebirth.

Game 5 back in K.C. wasn't exactly a formality.
That was, until, Big Ken's swing provided finality.

Another series won, another new opponent to face.
Birds from Canada who send balls into airspace.

The first was a whitewash, a shutout win.
Volquez and company as fans left with a grin.

The second looked much more dire.
That was until a pair of Jays disagreed on a flyer.

K.C. bats were then ready to swoop.
Moose and Gordon threw Price for a loop.

A commanding lead was taken north.
A place we know doesn't celebrate the Fourth.

These blue birds still had some pluck.
It's never too wise to doubt a Canuck.

Back to the States for hopefully the clincher.
Turned out Bautista was the flincher.

A wild sprint from over 270 feet.
Ended with a leap and a click of a cleat.

But even then, it wasn't even close to over.
The rain was concerning; would Wade be a holdover?

Tying run at third with nary an out,
Davis in his heart still never had a doubt.

And when yet another 5–3 was completed,
The American League pennant had been repeated.

The final climb on the mountain still hovered.
The big city Mets had those power arms covered.

A dash began the series and prophesized what was ahead.
But the Mets took a late lead and threatened some dread.

Familia was untouched, but Alex didn't care.
He sent that 97 mile-per-hour heater into the fall air.

Late into the night, the Mets D provided a chance.
A few minutes later, the Royals would dance.

Game 2 was about shimmy outbreaks,
As Johnny remained until the handshakes.

Noah, in Game 3, decided enough was enough.
He threw it high and tight, trying to be tough.

That game was forgettable and certainly not fun.
But turns out we were nice to at least give them one.

The next night proceeded as so many had done before.
The Royals waited until very late to roar.

A three-run eighth aided by an error.
A ball squirting under a glove, a city in terror.

And then, the night that we all had been waiting for.
A game and a team we'll dream about for days of yore.

A deficit again, not a surprise to this band.
A walk, a double, and then a dash so grand.

Scouting, a read, and a whole lot of daring,
Left those Mets fans in the crowd with a mouthful of swearing.

The game was tied but not yet won.
What remained was another moment from a "pick one."

C.C. was a winner; that's why he was here.
He was prepared despite inactivity and had no fear.

A 1–2 count, a single that will live forever.
A hit Dayton dreamed about during this 10-year endeavor.

When Cain found the gap, it was all but completed.
No fans of the Boys in Blue could remain seated.

Wade's final pitch froze our memories and that batter.
What followed next doesn't really matter.

Joy, elation, a completion of a wonderful quest.
Tears, smiles, the Royals were the best.

The trophy was raised, and Ned was soaked.
Comparisons were made, and the great clubs were invoked.

The party certainly lasted late into the New York night.
K.C. wasn't leaving this Big Apple without a big bite.

The next day seemed like a dream, but it was, oh, so concrete.
The bus ride home through a city with so much elation on the street.

The parade allowed nearly one million to share in the glory.
And every single one of the revelers had their own special story.

How they always believed, always were true.
How they never wavered from being Royal blue.

It was a day that will be talked about forever.
A day to be shared whenever, with whomever.

The journey was long and filled with many trials.
But it was all worth it to see all the smiles.

—*David Holtzman*

ACKNOWLEDGMENTS

Jeff Montgomery

To Matt Fulks, who did much of the heavy lifting during the process of writing this book. Thanks for lending your years of writing experience to this project. I couldn't have done this without you.

To everyone related to the Kansas City Royals for making Kansas City a great place to have a baseball career. Especially to all the players, coaches, managers, and trainers that I had the good fortune of playing this great game with for so many years.

To my current "teammates" at SportsRadio 810-WHB and FOX Sports Kansas City. Playing baseball is the greatest "job" in the world, but covering it on a daily basis as a member of the media is the second best "job" in the world. To my TV broadcast partner, Joel Goldberg, thanks for helping me so much, especially during the early years on TV.

As I mentioned in the dedication, I have many people to thank for their support during my career, but none more than my father, Tom Montgomery. I had many coaches throughout the years, but none that will ever appreciate me as much as my dad. He taught me more about baseball and life than anyone. Many of the lessons I've learned from him, I've tried to apply to my own life, especially as a husband and father.

Finally, to my wife, Tina, and our four wonderful children, Ashleigh, Connor, Spencer, and Katy, who mean more to me than anything in this world.

Matt Fulks

As always, there are too many people to thank because there's no way a book can be completed without a great amount of support and assistance. But, apologies if you're not mentioned by name. That said, the following people were incredibly instrumental in this book:

First and foremost, to Monty, who carved time out of his already hectic summer to make this book a reality. You say your memory isn't the best, but I think this book proves otherwise. It's been a pleasure and an honor to go on this journey with you.

To the team at Triumph Books, who believed in this project and kept pushing us forward: Josh Williams, Noah Amstadter, and our incredible editor Jeff Fedotin. Noah and Jeff have been stuck with me on multiple projects throughout my career, and they deserve a king's ransom for doing so.

To Royals general manager (as well as co-author and incredible boss with the "C" You In The Major Leagues Foundation) Dayton Moore for writing the foreword. To Dick Kaegel for writing the introduction. To have something written by Dick for this book is an undeserved honor for a hack like me.

To Mike Cummings and Mike Swanson in the Royals media relations department for your support and assistance with photos and information. To George Brett and Denny Matthews for allowing us to use your Baseball Hall of Fame speeches. To Dave Holtzman for allowing us to use your original poem about the Royals' renaissance.

To Jim Wissel, Chris Browne, Tom Lawrence, and Tim and Amy Brown, who are always a great core of support and guidance. As with past book projects, based on the amount of praying I did during the writing of this, especially during the last two weeks, without Christ this isn't possible.

A final special thanks to my favorite in-laws, Todd and Pat Burwell, and my parents, Fred and Sharon. To Helen, Charlie, and Aaron, who make me thankful each day, and, to my best friend, Libby, who loves me in spite of my Elvis habits and procrastination.

Thank you all.

SOURCES

The following were used to verify dates, statistics, and game information.

Books:

Matthews, Denny with Matt Fulks. *Tales from the Kansas City Royals Dugout.* New York: Skyhorse Publishing 2015.

Matthews, Denny with Matt Fulks. *Hi, Anybody!* Kansas City: Ascend Publishing 2009.

Moore, Dayton with Matt Fulks. *More Than A Season.* Chicago: Triumph Books 2015 (updated in 2016).

Periodicals:

The Kansas City Star
The New York Times
Royals Gameday (now *Royals Insider*)
USA TODAY

Websites:

baseballchronology.com
baseballhall.org
baseball-reference.com
bls.gov
businessinsider.com
royals.com
si.com

ABOUT THE AUTHORS

Jeff Montgomery spent 12 of his 13 big league seasons with the Royals and is the club's all-time saves leader with 304. The three-time All-Star (1992, 1993, 1996) was the Rolaids American League Reliever of the Year in 1993, finishing tied for the league lead with 45 saves, matching a club record at that time. "Monty" also holds the club record for career appearances (686) and ranked ninth on Major League Baseball's all-time saves list at the time of his retirement. In his eighth season contributing to Royals broadcasts on FOX Sports Kansas City, the Royals Hall of Famer serves as a co-host on *Royals Live* pregame and postgame shows. He also offers analysis in the broadcast booth during select games on FSKC. Montgomery is the vice president of Union Broadcasting, Inc. He lives in Kansas City with his wife, Tina, and four children: Ashleigh, Connor, Spencer, and Katy.

Matt Fulks started his journalism career while attending Lipscomb University in Nashville, Tennessee, when his baseball career was cut short due to a lack of ability. He is the author/co-author of more than 20 books, including projects with Dayton Moore, Denny Matthews, Frank White, and Fred White. The director of Moore's "C" You In The Major Leagues Foundation, Fulks lives in the Kansas City area with his wife, Libby, their three kids, his mid-life crisis Jeep, and two Weimaraners named after Elvis. Sort of. More info is available at MattFulks.com (about Matt's books, not the dogs).

Other Triumph Books titles by Matt Fulks

More Than a Season with Dayton Moore, 2015 (Updated in 2016)

Taking the Crown: The Kansas City Royals' Amazing 2015 Season, 2015

Out of the Blue: The Kansas City Royals' Historic 2014 Season, 2014

100 Things Chiefs Fans Should Know & Do Before They Die, 2014

100 Things Royals Fans Should Know & Do Before They Die, 2014
    (Updated in 2016)

Coach John Wooden: 100 Years of Greatness, 2010

The Good, the Bad, & the Ugly: Pittsburgh Steelers, 2008

Echoes of Kansas Basketball, 2006